CONCILIUM

THEOLOGY IN THE AGE OF RENEWAL

CONCILIUM

CONCILIUM / VOL. 19

SPIRITUALITY

SPIRITUALITY
IN THE
SECULAR
CITY

Volume 19

CONCILIUM
theology in the age of renewal

PAULIST PRESS
NEW YORK, N.Y. / GLEN ROCK, N.J.

NIHIL OBSTAT: Joseph F. Donahue, S.J., S.T.L.
Censor Deputatus

IMPRIMATUR: ✠ Bernard J. Flanagan, D.D.
Bishop of Worcester

October 28, 1966

The Nihil Obstat and Imprimatur are official declarations that a book or pamphlet is free of doctrinal or moral error. No implication is contained therein that those who have granted the Nihil Obstat and Imprimatur agree with the contents, opinions or statements expressed.

Library of Congress Catalogue Card Number: 66-30386

Suggested Decimal Classification: 291.4

BOOK DESIGN: Claude Ponsot

Paulist Press assumes responsibility for the accuracy of the English translations in this Volume.

PAULIST PRESS
EXECUTIVE OFFICES: 304 W. 58th Street, New York, N.Y. and 21 Harristown Road, Glen Rock, N.J.
Executive Publisher: John A. Carr, C.S.P.
Executive Manager: Alvin A. Illig, C.S.P.
Asst. Executive Manager: Thomas E. Comber, C.S.P.

EDITORIAL OFFICES: 304 W. 58th Street, New York, N.Y.
Editor: Kevin A. Lynch, C.S.P.
Managing Editor: Urban P. Intondi

Printed and bound in the United States of America by
The Colonial Press Inc., Clinton, Mass.

CONTENTS

PART II

BIBLIOGRAPHICAL SURVEY

PART III

DO-C DOCUMENTATION CONCILIUM

PART I
ARTICLES

Michel de Certeau, S.J./*Paris, France*

Culture and Spiritual Experience

P resent-day studies on the history of the spiritual life seem at first sight to present the reader with a somewhat paradoxical scene. The writers take two opposite positions quite unlike what would have been expected. In the one camp are those who are chiefly concerned with religion. They underline the unfortunate rift between the spiritual life and "the world" of contemporary cultures, and they tend to look for the genuine expression of the spiritual life outside this "spiritual" language, and in any case beyond this rift. In the other camp are the historians who work along socio-cultural lines and do not share these views, which they claim to be still imbued with a dogmatic dualism. Within the orbit of a particular language and within the framework of society, spirituality would rather seem to them to be something brought to the surface by the deep underground currents that successively give birth to the realms of ideas.

In effect, both these camps are looking at the matter through the same spectacles. Their contemporary outlook conditions their attitude to the past. But we must give them credit here for a genuinely spiritual concern, for every generation enters into debate with its predecessors and takes upon itself to choose the ground. In our generation, this might well be determined by the thousand and one pointers toward an "anthropology" [1] or science of man. Where does man stand? What is the truth about man? What is his history and what risks confront him in the future? The urgency of these questions would equally explain the wide divergence between the attitudes to spirituality, when it comes under the suspicion of despising culture, and the tendency to look upon it simply as a particular mode of human language.

But this problem of the essential approach takes on wider ramifications, for each analysis is bound to be proportionate to its predecessors and to an historical background that not only is the object of research, but also conditions that research. The approach will therefore vary according as the historian's background is a scientific positivism that rules out the spiritual, or a spiritual outlook that would look upon the spiritual world as the only genuine witness to the true nature of man. From this point of view, the scrutiny of the past centuries is seen to imply an immediate past that is shared by the historian; and the present-day anthropological outlook, common to all, involves a particular method of interrogating and, therefore, of interpreting all spiritual material.

When he includes spiritual literature as a part of culture, or when he distinguishes the one from the other in order to define their relationship more precisely, the author carrying out this scrutiny takes up his position according to his own past and is himself determined by it. In his very anxiety to be fair (typical of our age) and in his own particular way of embodying it in a method (belonging to a specific environment), he is giving cultural expression to a spiritual question even when he is making judgments on situations in the past and historical relationships between culture and the spiritual world. The way the question is formulated is therefore germane to the problem that confronts us. In terms of our present culture, it stands for a series of questions about men. In order to analyze the relations between cul-

---

[1] Cf. P. Rivet, "Lettre à 'Diogène' sur l'évolution du sens du mot Anthropologie," in *Diogène* 13 (1956), pp. 140-43.

ture and the spiritual world, it is important to realize that the very question betrays a good deal about its proper object. An analysis of the problems that are present may therefore be made more accurate by a consideration of the existing links between culture and the spiritual life.

I

THE SPIRITUAL LIFE IN THE LIGHT OF CULTURE

History and Culture

To read about the past is always in fact to ask questions about the present, as can be seen in the two outlooks we have taken as our starting point. Some maintain that the business of historical analysis is to capture the self-awareness of a particular past society and so display the unity-in-diversity of the social symbolism to which a *Geistgeschichte* is constantly pointing. Here, the multiple aspects of cultural "communication", including the spiritual world, cutting across conscious ideas, thought-forms, underlying postulates or sensory perception, are, so to speak, so many "stops" in the use of a language. All these "synchronistic" aspects are related to the mental "coherence" of the collective psyche. In reaction against a science that is preoccupied and almost obsessed by cultural "objects", this is a viewpoint that restores to language its true significance, seeing in it an exchange of goods and words, a social circulation, a reciprocal "intercourse" that works out its "values" on the basis of truths held in common and takes for granted a pool of common interests.[2]

And so there emerges, tacitly underlying all the dialogue, an implicit solidarity. What is left unsaid is as important as what is said; in human thought, it is the "unspoken thought" which

[2] It will be sufficient here to refer to the works of C. Lévi-Strauss, particularly, in his *Anthropologie structurale* (Paris, 1958), the chapters entitled "Histoire et ethnologie" and "Langage et société"), or, from a very different viewpoint, the essays of A. Dupront: for example, "Problèmes et méthodes d'une histoire de la psychologie collective," in *Annales E.S.C.* 16 (1961).

comes in to systematize it and leave it henceforward sitting rather loose to language and so open to the task of rethinking.[3]

To be sure, this idea of a "social coherence", "complex", "mentality" or "specific collective" is only valid because it has been found to "work". It is an analytical tool that is neither obvious nor clearly defined *per se,* but which is necessary for the understanding of history. It brings out the time-links between different mental systems and the spiritual experiences enshrined in them. For every spiritual reaction, before being either an act of refusal or an act of adhesion, is a *fact* of adaptation. "Experience is always defined in cultural terms, even when it is religious!" [4] It responds, and so makes an adjustment, to the total situation. Even the signs of protest, such as a "cleavage", or a "return to the primitive beliefs", take on a form that is necessarily related to the problems of society as a whole. Both in his "contempt" and in his isolation, the faithful soul is still dependent on the thing that he is fighting against; in fact it is new ways of thought (though clothed in the garb of yesterday) that will determine what he holds as immutable and the way in which he will affirm it and live it out. His ideas are provided by the present, although he thinks that by inverting them he is turning his back on them.

Culture and Spiritual Movements

Every culture is thus provided with an excellent signpost in the shape of the great spiritual movements strewn along the path of its history, represented by the new problems thrown up in the evolution of a society, its stresses and its aspirations, which explode in huge religious drives. Thus, in the Middle Ages you have the Crusades, running through the length and breadth of the land, extending into foreign parts and leaving their mark on history. They are a "political sublimation", an expression of the elementary and vital needs of the collective being, a panic

[3] M. Foucault, *Naissance de la clinique* (Paris, 1965), XV.
[4] M.-J. Herskovits, *Cultural Anthropology* (New York: Knopf, 1955).

action to ensure a common salvation.[5] In the same way the approval given to spiritual "poverty" and the critical attitude that later replaced it went hand in hand with a collective uprooting of all ties, which first brought renewal, and then shook the foundations, in an entire society.[6] In the 16th century, groups of "illuminati" (Alumbrados, Recogidos or Dejados), fascinated by subjective experiences, were witnesses to the path leading from angelology and cosmology to a religious psychology that lies on the further side of a disenchantment with religious tradition.[7] In the mid-18th century, while politics were becoming the affair of the layman, spiritual "societies" arose on the fringes of the Church that gave expression to a "mystical life" standing apart from the objective rules imposed by Christian institutions or by the royal good pleasure.[8] This was a prelude to the "devoutness" that was to react to the "age of enlightenment" by institutions such as the "assembly of fools". And in our day, the Jamaa movement has all the spiritual greatness belonging to an historic hour in the history of the Congo. Its religious features betray the problems of decolonization at the precise moment when it was an inevitable reaction to what had gone before. The relationships between the priest and the faithful then became inverted, and so through them the relationship of black and white, man and woman, technical advance and custom, Western institutions and ancestral traditions, the merely notional and the "vital", without it being possible for anyone with an eye to the future to assume that at this point two different historical streams have come together.

[5] Cf. P. Alphandéry and A. Dupront, La chrétienté et l'idée de croisade (Paris, 1954-1959), pp. 273-89.

[6] We refer to the research directed by M. Mollat at the Sorbonne (Paris) since 1962 "on the poor and poverty in the Middle Ages" and on the relation of spirituality to this circle of ideas.

[7] Cf. the numerous studies by L. Sala Balust, particularly En torno al grupo de Alumbrados de Llenera (Madrid, 1965), or the latest work by A. Selke de Sanchez in the Bulletin Hispanique.

[8] Cf. M. de Certeau, "Politique et mystique," in Rev. asc. myst. 39 (1963), pp. 45-82.

II

SPIRITUAL LANGUAGES AND LANGUAGES OF A PARTICULAR TIME

In these various cases, the language of a particular cultural moment is brought into use again in a "spiritual" setting, but this implies a constellation of other forms of expression, analogous or different, although always "coherent" in relation to the whole. The structures of society, the terms in which it voices its aspirations, the objective and subjective forms of the common conscience, build up the religious conscience, which in turn manifests them. A particular type of society and a particular social balance (including the essential elements of the significance of power, the social conception of marriage, etc.) are reflected in the problems of spiritual experience. And, what is more, the elaboration of a spiritual system at the center of a collective movement leads in its turn to a reinterpretation of the most traditional ideas (such as those of father, mother, wife, king, love, etc.), along with the whole "spiritual" vocabulary. The same words, the same ideas and the same definitions then cease to have the same significance or the same function in the new language into which they have been taken up and transposed in a more or less perceptible manner.

Looking at the matter from an analogous standpoint, one can hardly fail to see in the 17th century the mental connection between the shaking to its foundations of a Christian civilization intent upon rediscovering the certainty of "objects" on the one hand, and on the other, the glorification of eucharistic realism, or the part played by the displaying of the host to human sight and taste. Or again, in the 19th century, the "introdetermined" society[9] founded upon the principles of moral autonomy on the one hand, and, on the other, the increasing stress laid upon the idea of culpability and the place of confession in the religious life. Or again, in the 20th century, the "extrodetermined" structure of a conscience that inclines to socialism, spurred on by the

---

[9] We refer to the ideas worked out by D. Riesman in *Faces in the Crowd* (New Haven: Yale University Press, 1952).

painful anxiety to be "with it" on the one hand, and, on the other, the part played by the team, by the elements of encounter or dialogue, even in the communion liturgy. Surely at all these different periods we can trace cross references and coherencies between those various movements: between the daring deeds of the conquering explorer in search of "rarities" and the mystic's journey marked with its "extraordinary" experiences; between the colonizer's mentality and the missionary's spiritual outlook; between the recognition of the social question and the spiritual themes of the working man, Nazareth and the modern "poor".

Perhaps it will be said that all this implies a very external view of things and a very superficial look at spiritual experience through the distorting spectacles of a sociology of religions or a history of the religious "sentiment" taken in isolation. But the essentials cannot be thus separated from the phenomena, for the latter conditions the form that conscience takes and structures the essential experiences of Christians and even of mystics. In order to affirm that there is an *essential core* in experience we should have to maintain that a part of its vocabulary is unchanging. But both history and sociology rule out any such superficial view, for they show only too clearly that these very words have been subject to great variations in meaning and relationship. No, the essential element in any spiritual experience is not some "otherness" quite outside the language of the time. This very language is what the spiritual man takes seriously; it is in this very cultural situation that his yearnings and his predicament "take flesh"; it is through this medium that he finds God, yet ever seeks him, that he expresses his faith, that he carries on simultaneous experiments in colloquy with God and with his actual brothers.

II

The Historicity of Spiritual Experience

A culture is the language of a spiritual experience. The very history of spirituality demonstrates this fact, unless we are determined to look at it with blinkers and thus exclude its context. And by "context" I mean not only a framework or external trappings, but the very element from which the experience takes its form and its expression. The problem is on each occasion defined by a cultural dialectic—the problem that the "spiritual" man will see as that of his union with God. Spiritual experience replies to the questions of the moment, and always replies in the terms of those questions, for these are what the men of a particular society talk about and live by—Christians as much as any others.

Because it is often describing an experience, and because in any case it has in mind the difficulties of actually living out any practice of religion, every spiritual movement is essentially historical in character. It is less concerned with elaborating a theory than with showing how to live in dependence on the Absolute in the conditions actually laid down by a given cultural situation. It is therefore expressed in terms of the experiences, ambitions, fears, sicknesses and greatnesses proper to men who are caught up with contemporaries in a world conditioned by a particular kind of exchange and a particular type of consciousness. An example may serve to bring this out better than any general considerations.

The 16th and 17th Centuries: A New Problem

Thus the spirituality of the 16th and 17th centuries is inseparable from the "crisis" that changed the face of the whole of Western civilization and renewed its mental horizons, its intellectual criteria and its social order (which is, in the ultimate analysis, its "reason").[10] A whole universe crumbled to ruin.

[10] Cf. especially R. Mousnier, *Les XVIe et XVIIe siècles* (Paris,

The religious wars brought a relative element into man's convictions; the proliferation of Churches split up the homogeneous nature of men's securities, both religious and mental; the peasant revolts, famines and epidemics all bore witness to and accentuated the disarray of political structures. Men experienced nature as a mighty and omnipresent tide which was all-powerful and swept all before it; it filled them with a magical and monstrous life, the "only force to maintain its strength and vitality in the disorder and collapse of institutions, doctrines and beliefs, in spite of all hindrances and in the face of all opposition".[11] The widespread existence of fear is equally to be seen in the social aggressiveness of groups, in the hypersensitivity of individuals, which could be both maudlin and cruel, both ambitious and super-subtle,[12] and, finally, in the underground demonological urges which tried to localize the unnamable menace by sacrificing "sorcerers" and "witches" who had no means of disproving this designation and whose agonies of suffering often seemed to suggest their guilt. Furthermore, the discovery of new races of men, hitherto unknown, opened the way, through the apologia on behalf of "the noble savage" and "the wise Chinaman", to a questioning of traditional values and lowered the credit of the intellectual and religious teachings which had come down from the past.[13] Scientific discoveries moved in the same direction. In astronomy, they shattered the "cozy little world" whose internal organization was proof of divine providence and an ascending spiritual ladder from sphere to sphere, from the terrestrial concavity of the cosmos right up to the empyrean.[14]

---

[9] 1961); R. Mandrou, *Introduction à la France moderne, 1500-1640* (Paris, 1961); M. Foucauld, *Folie et déraison. Histoire de la folie à l'âge classique* (Paris, 1961).

[11] A. Koyré, *Mystiques, spirituels, alchimistes du XVIe siècle allemand* (Paris, 1955), pp. 50-51.

[12] Cf. R. Mandrou, *op. cit.*, pp. 336-46.

[13] Cf. G. Atkinson, *Extraordinary Voyage in French Literature,* 2 Vols., Vol. 1 before 1700 (New York, 1964).

[14] Cf. A. Koyré, *Du monde clos à l'univers infini* (Paris, 1962); R. Lenoble, "L'évolution de l'idée de nature du XVIe au XVIIIe siècle," *Rev. de métaphysique et de morale,* 58 (1953), pp. 108-29; P.-H. Michel, "La querelle du géocentrisme," in *Studi Secenteschi,* II/1 (1962), pp. 95-118.

A world-scheme in ruin, or a sheer vacuum—both were equally powerful in removing the sense of mystery from man's knowledge and man's abilities.

Nevertheless, this reduction of status was the reverse side of a new cultural creation. "Man at this time was a traveler who was no longer astray *in* the world, but rather a traveler led astray *by* the world." [15] Because he had lost the cosmos that had been the framework of his existence and the object of his knowledge, he was driven back to search for certainty and order *in himself*. Through all the cult of skepticism and stoicism, through all the criticism of tradition and institutionalism, there emerges always and everywhere this question of the subject, this question of an autonomy which is both a witness to and a creator of reason, this question of an individuality that is a "world" by itself, and the truth about the world as *thought*.

This whole cultural turnabout was expressed in a literature of *illusion;* reality was as fugitive, changing, iridescent and fragile as a bubble, constantly taking on new shapes. It was without any consistency; the heavens followed the movements of Borromini's cupolas dissolving and revolving as though caught up in a fit of cosmic vertigo; the earth was only a stage built up from flattering but futile "appearances"—"a mad world", as Thomas Middleton called it. And the logic of this "vanity" was indefinite, for there was never anything behind "appearance" but another "appearance". Although the management might slyly invite the spectator to come behind the scenes and see what went on in the wings, he would never find anything at the back of the show but another stage setting.[16] The marvels set forth in the novels could only hold up before him a mirror that reflected his own confusion as he read of the "paradises" described by so many literary[17] or spiritual works of the period. Among many

[15] P.-H. Michel, *op. cit.*, p. 110.
[16] R. Alewyn, *L'univers baroque* (Paris, 1964), pp. 92-98; Ger. tr.: *Das Grosse Welttheater* (Hamburg, 1959). Cf. also J. Rousset, *La littérature à l'âge baroque en France* (Paris,³1960).
[17] Cf. J. Ehrmann, *Un paradis désespéré. L'amour et l'illusion dans "L'Astrée"* (Paris-New Haven, 1963).

thousands, we might select the doctor and chemist Jean-Baptiste Van Helmont (1577-1644) as a good exponent of this questioning mood, when he sees, in a dream that already has a Cartesian flavor, the cosmos appear as a "vain bubble" floating above a "dark abyss". He resolves to seek the criterion of certainty in experience alone, and he sweeps away the structure of this illusory cosmos to place in the "center" of human life (but no longer at the head of the universe) the principle of man's biological and spiritual life.[18]

The Mysticism of an Age: Teresa of Avila

Nor did the exponents of the spiritual life speak a very different language. It would therefore be wrong to reproach them with having lived out the drama of the age, for that was precisely where their problem lay. They saw it and thought about it by reason of their sensitivity and their participation in common ways of thought, but they also looked upon it as a meeting point with the God who always reveals his truth as a truth about man. And so nothing comes closer to Van Helmont's philosophical dream than the visions and illuminations of his contemporary mystics. To remind ourselves of the most famous of them, it will be enough to mention the vision related by St. Teresa at the beginning of *The Interior Castles,* which she holds to be "the theme [motive] and foundation of this book", her great treatise on mysticism.[19] The symbolism is expressive of the structure to which the thought refers, although it does not succeed in making it entirely explicit. In this respect it is particularly revealing. With Teresa, the symbolism is still cosmological, for it does in effect take up the structure of the universe as described by Peter

---

[18] J.-B. Van Helmont, "Confessio authoris," in *Ortus medicinae* (Amsterdam, 1652).

[19] *Moradas del Castillo interior,* Vol. 1, chapters 1-2: in *Obras Completas* (Madrid: BAC, 1954), pp. 341-43, 348-49; Eng. tr. in *The Complete Works of St. Teresa of Jesus,* ed. E. Addison Peers (London: Sheed and Ward, 1948). This idea of St. Teresa's dates from June 2, 1577. For the event and its literary sources, cf. Efren de la Madre de Dios, *ibid.,* pp. 311-14, and, above all, R. Ricard, "Le symbolisme du 'château intérieur' chez Sainte Thérèse," in *Bulletin hispanique* 67 (1965), pp. 25-41.

Appianas in his *Cosmographia* (1539). At the center there is the earth, surrounded by the spheres defined by the orbits of the moon, Mercury, Venus, the sun and so on up to the ninth and tenth heavens, the whole being encompassed by the "Coelum empireum habitaculum Dei et omnium electorum".[20] But here, this scheme of things is exactly reversed. St. Teresa's symbolical theme is no longer concerned with the structure of a cosmic *object,* but with a cosmic *subject:* it transposes the old cosmology into the form of anthropology. The cosmos is now represented with earth at its lower point, the earth on which the celestial influx descends and from which the soul rises to return to the *empireum,* and this cosmos becomes a human microcosm, a "globe" like the ancient world and "clear as crystal" like the bubble. This is a world that is constituted by each single person, whose center is the "mansion" of God, a world that is surrounded by "the dark abyss". In St. Teresa's vision, the concentric circles of the old cosmology are also still in the picture, but now they mark the interior development of the soul which is due to the "sun" within the human heart, and no longer an ascent through a series of heavens.

And so the globe becomes the *new* language of mystical experience, but not in the sense that this constitutes a hitherto unpublished picture or idea, for the metaphor of the "mansion" and the "center" is a traditional one, and that of the "castle" surrounded by ramparts had a previous history in the 16th century which would have been well-known to St. Teresa. What is new is the all-embracing part played by the cultural movement of disintegration and innovation, significant because it sums up much past history and represents the cultural and spiritual structure of a new mystical awareness. The symbol stands both for what is perishing and for what is being born. The deterioration of one universe becomes for St. Teresa the language of another universe, that of anthropology. The confusions that were depriving man of his world and at the same time of the objective signs of God's activity are seen to be the very ground of his spiritual

---

[20] Cf. A. Koyré, *Du monde clos à l'univers infini, op. cit.,* p. 31.

rebirth. This is the place where the faithful will find the sure token of God, with a certainty that will henceforth be founded upon a consciousness of self. Man discovers in himself what transcends self and roots him firmly in existence.

But there was more than this. Henceforward, his history would no longer consist of passing through objective stages of progress or be measured by objects of a cosmological or religious order. It would consist of a journey into oneself. Spiritual progress would be the way taken by man to arrive at his own center. This was a concept that answered the problem of the time, but it was in keeping with the terms in which it was presented. Man could now become spiritually aware by grasping a truth which created before his eyes an "objectivity", the "vanity" of all the exterior world. This reciprocal demarcation of an "interior" and "exterior" which then became part and parcel of religious experience explains the tremendous part played by the word *mystic* in the 17th century. The word stood for a journey no longer thought of in terms of a visible advance from place to place, or by an increase in knowledge, but now envisaged as a "becoming", clothed in stable religious language, yet not subject to the transitoriness of things. It was to be a secret mutation, grasped and recognized by virtue of a disenchantment with the universe of words, ideas or objective certainties.[21] And in the vision of mystical theology, this "becoming" was to have one single meaning: it was to stand for the principle of a continual "reaching out", because truth is the "center" which never ceases to attract the soul as it reveals itself, and thus builds up the inner man through all the multifarious events, decisions and loyalties that mark the path of life.

Questions about Man Are Spiritual Questions

In these particular respects, the experience of the mystics was analogous to that of the boldest of their contemporaries. Des-

[21] M. de Certeau, " 'Mystique' au XVIIe siècle. Le problème du langage 'mystique,' " in *L'homme devant Dieu* (Paris, 1964), pp. 267-91.

cartes, who had set out "as a man walking alone in darkness", [22] was for his part to discover in his *cogito* the innateness of the idea of God, and with him, as with the mystics, the form in which he set out his ideas was a measure of their content. He put forward the *Discourse on Method* as an intellectual biography, "a personal history",[23] which was intended to reconstruct the order of a universe by starting out from a *perceptio* of the infinite in the self. The biographies of the spiritually preeminent are similar in range, inspired by the same root question (that of the subject) and guided by the same criteria (the experiences that mark out the path of a personal discovery). It would therefore be a profound mistake not to see the essential problem of a whole culture in the "psychological" vocabulary used by the mystics, which often leads us astray as to the true sense of their words, just as it proved a snare to the lesser spirits among them too.

Such similar lines could not be explained as merely a matter of influence; they are related to a question posed by a cultural situation and made explicit in a common language. They bear witness to the existence of a great contemporary problem at this period, which explains why the imagery as well as the presentation of the problems evolves in step with the culture. With the mystics, the "microcosmological" pattern is only predominant for a fairly short time, while they are passing through a mental revolution. Soon—from the middle of the 17th century onward —this "microcosmic" imagery disappears, and so do the "natural" references. They are succeeded by religious language in a social and technical key, in which the vocabulary of the "natural" elements is replaced by a reversion to the symbolism of a social order then coming into being (the functions of a king, the relations between the "court" and the city, the status and the prejudices which define the relationships between social bodies, the conception of marriage, etc.). With increasing frequency it

[22] *Discours de la méthode,* 1: in *Oeuvres* (ed. Adam and Tannery), 6, 16.

[23] *Ibid.,* p. 4.

is technical activities (such as spinning, astronomy, etc.) that furnish the language of the spiritual quest. In the same way, union with God revolves from this time onward around the elements and the symbolism of social relations,[24] whereas it was previously expressed as the soul's urgent need for a new grasp of God, and earlier still as the interiorization of a tradition that had been handed on by previous generations. The evolution of the spiritual vocabulary followed the experiences of culture because spiritual experience was altogether bound up with the questions presented to man by his history and by his collective awareness of them, but its evolution was bound to be here and nowhere else.

III

SPIRITUAL "RUPTURES"

Experience

But this likeness, even if it is obvious or at any rate demonstrable, is not sufficient to account for everything. Within a collective system, spiritual thought puts forward a special characteristic which it designates as "experience" and circumscribes with such specific labels as "the science of experience", "practical" wisdom, and the literature of "the existential". But experience runs some risk of being an equivocal term. One cannot understand it in the sense in which it would be properly applicable to the spiritual life alone or in the sense in which it would imply something beyond the sphere of language. On the one hand, this experience is itself defined by the type of expression referring to it and distinguishing it from other "sciences" (theological, philosophical, physical, etc.) which are likewise closely bound up with experience. On the other hand, what is called the ineffable is in reality a particular kind of discourse, a spiritual language; although it refuses other languages such as that of theology, it does not refuse all languages as such.

[24] Cf. J.-J. Surin, *Correspondance* (1966), pp. 51-56.

In the references to "the ineffable", the negative is only directed against particular forms of expression—the intellectual, for instance. But there is no language that does not constitute and express an experience, whether it be of a discursive, descriptive or dialectical character. Inversely, there is no experience that does not express itself in language, or that is not—at a deeper level—itself a language, even if it be only the language of intuition. Experience then is neither specific to language nor exclusive of language. In this respect, it is insufficient for the definition of specific character. It cannot be more than an indication of it, whose meaning must be sought in the part played by the need to speak of it and the way in which it is spoken of, as well as in the function of this resort.

The "Rupture"

We come back then to this aspect of difference or rift which up till now we have had to consider within a cultural *continuum*. A "rupture" is a constant element in the spiritual life, and can already be seen in the privilege granted to experience. To be sure, the specific thing is not the experience but the fact that it should be "spiritual". Moreover, the "rupture" is not something that can be isolated in the necessarily collective language of the spiritual life. It belongs to the "style" of this language. Perhaps the element that is essentially characteristic of the "rupture" is *surprise*. It is immanent in the spiritual attitude, but it increases in proportion to the boldness of the faith that God initiates, sustains and dashes to the ground always through the instrumentality of some human pattern of events. This boldness may assume different forms, but it always consists of being ready to go to the extreme point in the tensions and ambitions belonging to a particular time, and of taking seriously a network of relationships in order to await and recognize in them the coming of God. This serious outlook may even be the origin of the Christian's dismay. When he launches out in full faith and with all his heart into human history, he is surprised that he is met with a "vacuum", as much on the part of religious teaching as in the activities and the knowledge which could yet, in a given situation, provide a meeting point with God.

The "Rupture" in Relation to Tradition

On the one hand, religious tradition reveals a certain defect in respect of the light one might have expected from it. This defect will be blamed on the faithful soul or on theology according to the cultural context, inasmuch as it engenders confidence in the object of faith or in the believer, and it will be held to indicate something missing in the one or the other. But justifiable as they may be, those explanations are an indication of a more radical fault. There is no correspondence between the evangelical word to which the believer replies and the response he hopes to find in it. This is the first form taken by the "rupture". This is a trial that comes to any Christian—today, yesterday or in the past—who is pledged to the word he has given. And so, in days gone by, certain brave and faithful women came in the small hours to visit the place where Jesus *should* have been lying as an object and a sign, but they discovered an "empty" tomb and they were filled with "amazement" (Mk. 16, 5-7). What Christian is there who has not been filled with amazement at some similar "emptiness"?

This trial will either bring out a sense of guilt or it will provoke criticism; it may lead to dismay or to protest. But in the first place it is a fact that has many resemblances to the experience of Job. When discussing the truths coming to him from his friends and his forebears, Job laid bare to the point of nakedness the "vanity" of a tradition that was nothing more than intellectual knowledge. You offer me truths (he said in effect), but they are mere generalities; what relationship have they to my present situation? They disappoint my expectations because they know nothing of my case. Mere truths are empty and useless—one cannot live on them. Even if recognized to be valid in themselves, and perhaps in this respect irreproachable (which is far from being always the case), the words of the wise and the learned are disappointing because they do not fit the question. It is therefore not surprising that the spiritual person, disappointed as Descartes was "by the terms of ordinary language",[25] should, like St. Teresa, seek for "new words" (*nuevas palabras*).[26] This initial surprise is where a "rupture" takes place; it already marks the formation of a specific language and determines the meaning it will give to "experience". This is a constant occurrence in spiritual history, but it takes on a more acute form in the recent dissensions between the spiritually minded and theologians.[27]

It would be a great misunderstanding of this "rupture" to see it only as a symptom of psychological fixations, or as a gulf between the life lived and the doctrine believed, between the particularism of the one and the universalism of the other. For the solitude of the Christian over against his own tradition is the reverse side of a certain solidarity, a sharing in a kind of language that has not been put into Gospel terms. The "spiritual person's" disappointment is expressed in a language that has not yet acquired or created its Christian punctuation. With all its impurities, lack of balance or illusion (aspects that are all bound up with the needs, problems and forms of conscience, etc.), it nevertheless testifies to a faith which knows that it must find God in the place where questions are being asked about man, and which refuses to treat the insufficiency of religious signs as a proof of the absence of God. True, it is partly the picture a Christian forms of theology that creates the gulf. But at a deeper level, why then does his present—his native land—consider itself to be "another world" from that of orthodox religious teaching, if not because it is new and a stranger to the cultures that God has already ordained? The Christian has thrown himself into a region where there are always risks to be run and new beginnings to be made. In relation to his religious knowledge, this is his "wilderness", a wilderness which is nowadays represented by his

---

[25] *Méditations*, II, 8: in *Oeuvres* (ed. Adam and Tannery), 9, I, 25; 7, 32.

[26] *Vida*, 25: in *Obras* 1 (Madrid: BAC, 1951), p. 748.

[27] Cf. F. Vandenbroucke, "Le divorce entre théologie et mystique," in *Nouv. Rev. Théol.* 72 (1950), pp. 372-89; Y. Congar, "Langage des spirituels et langage des théologiens," in *La mystique rhénane* (Paris, 1963), pp. 15-34.

town and the zone of changing culture in which he lives. In this respect, the gap that separates the believer from his theology is in fact an advance beyond it that he has achieved in the narrow field of a particular and personal experience. He devotes it all to a task that the situation presents him with, and the gulf that yawns is the measure of his boldness. It can even be the sign of a faith that is working out its own symbolism from its new mental outlook, although the symbolism is as yet only negative, something snatched up in the absence of theology, or when theology lags far behind—as it must seem from the necessarily narrow, but nonetheless real, territory occupied by experience. A certain sense of human "belonging" would seem to be the proper language of a spiritual experience.

The "Rupture" in Relation to the World

On the other hand, a gulf can also open up in the midst of this sense of belonging. It can even split the feeling of "solidarity" which created a sense of "apartness" with regard to the language of religion. This new aspect invests the relationship testified to by the former. What a man has recognized as necessary and vital in the preaching of the faith, he now seeks for in his relationships and his work as a human being; but just where he *ought* to find this, he discovers a new form of "something lacking". He experiences a disappointment which conjures up before itself an object called "the world". In the network of his human intercourse, in pursuing the lines of his investigation, he was always hoping to see some unforeseeable, yet familiar face. All the works of human communication are signs that renew his question, "Where hast thou hidden thyself?", although they do not supply an answer. They voice nothing but his longings. He comes to hope for more from these "messengers" than they can give, until such time as he discovers their message about others and about himself in the very disappointments they bring: "None of them can tell me what I am looking for." [28]

As in the previous cases, this sense of disappointment wit-

[28] St. John of the Cross, *Cantique spirituel*, str. 1 and 6.

nesses to a new step forward and a new encounter. Faith is the discovery which recognizes in everyday language that there is Someone speaking to whom one can reply. It is thus already aware that all human speech has a divine meaning. Just as the language of faith is led up to by the real experience of the believer, so their works and quests as human beings are constantly being called in question and interrogated by the certainty this language has revealed to them. It is true that this certainty is still negative in character, in spite of its being so clear. It is based upon a Presence who makes himself known by calling this assurance in question, by opening up, in the very quick of existence, the sense of the needs of others, and by revealing himself as that without which life is impossible: "To whom then shall we go? For thou hast the words of eternal life" (Jn. 6, 68). But however "eternal" and unapproachable this "life" may be, it is nonetheless brought to the believer by a tradition, a religious teaching, a Church—realities that are rooted in history and society. But the certainty of faith already speaks its own language; it must then be in the name of catechetical or theological knowledge, liturgical experience or meditation on the scriptures, that an equally necessary criticism takes shape, leading to a tension —in the double sense of the word. This faith speaks prophetically of a Presence who is both immediately felt and yet still to come, who cannot be refused without a betrayal of all language, and yet who cannot be immediately grasped and held in the terms of any particular language.

The Sense of a Double "Rupture"

With this double "rupture" there accordingly appears a dialectical movement not only at work within each culture, but also leading to an unceasing "dialogue" between its particular forms. Mutual criticism is the form this encounter assumes. The two contradictory moments of the experience set up a *movement* which cannot be identified with any one of its terms or landmarks. In each of the sectors where the Christian would think he could, or ought to, pin down truth, there is always a certain "swing back" to another balancing truth, tarnishing the successive objects to which he clings. And the "disappointment" he feels in relation to each of them is an echo of this confrontation. The "rupture" is the form taken by a reciprocal sense of dependence; it is the "outside"—and perhaps the only expressible part —of the way to God.

A cultural pluralism is here the element in the spiritual journey which already aims at unity, although it forbids the assigning of it to any particular country, which unmasks the hope of a pure and simple "beyond", although it affirms a truth that has already been vouchsafed in the very process of seeking for it, and which forms the conscious history of the renewals that have been brought about by this very difference. At the heart of a single culture, languages take on a symbolical character when, by coming together, they reveal a truth about each person which he would have been unable to express by himself. Truth is never expressible in any terms other than historical. It is always more than the "I" or the "we" who speaks it. He who receives it is, as it were, snatched away from his very self; it can be recognized by the wound that opens up into language even where truth was already being revealed. The theology of experience (which gathers the sense because it is immanent in a given language) can only be a theology of distance (that is, of privation brought about by the presence of the other). Its expression is always relative to the situation in which there arises, like a summons, the telltale "lack" of a symbolism linking different languages which are all necessary for the manifestation of what is true.

Each spiritual system expresses this reciprocity in the cultural element, even up to the very manner in which it causes a swing in the opposite direction. The solitude of the Egyptian hermit in his desert constantly sends his thoughts back to the city of Alexandria and to the merchant who is holier than he; the medieval abbey cannot help thinking of the miseries of the age and the necessities of contemporary politics; the mystical psychology of St. Teresa cannot but contemplate the dramatic events set in train by the progressive dissolution of Christianity. Each form of "rupture" has to find its own true meaning in the demand that it makes for an interior progress beyond the very heart of the "rupture" itself. Division even creeps into the position that puts forth bold views as to the way that a separation or a departure should be made. For the desert father, there is no "solitude" or "good works" that can guarantee faithfulness to the Spirit; for the spiritual man of the 16th century, there is no "notion" or "vision" that can be identified with the knowledge or the will of God. No "return to the Gospel" can assure him that he is hearing the true Word. Never can the spiritual man point in any way whatsoever to "the situation of an earthly paradise" on the map.[29] He learns how to recognize "paradise" in the banishment from his true home that is demanded from him, in respect of the place where he finds himself, by those very people he has left in order to go and find it.

He goes through all the possibilities of experience offered by his time, taking up a particular one to express something that stands for his spiritual quest and ambition; but this something is snatched away from him by what others show him of the nature of his desire. He moves through experiences like an itinerant traveler, and his luggage follows along roads opened up by human traffic, but it only contains a limited series of cultural elements, for his luggage is no richer than that of his contemporaries. But what he gives to them and receives from them in the course of the exchanges which take place even in the most secret depths of his conscience, even in the "temptations" and "calls" still voiced in him by the language of others—all this he seizes upon as a question reopened by each encounter, as a welcome wound in the heart of all human and religious solidarity, as a Presence whom no absences and no new stages of experience have ever fully spelled out.

[29] This is the title of a work by D. Huet, *Traité de la situation du paradis terrestre*, "avec une carte".

IV

CULTURAL AND SPIRITUAL FIXATIONS

The mistake does not lie in adding to a cultural exchange a repartee which discovers or defends a particular religious position. For these reactions or "ruptures" are part of the necessary movement, thanks to which progress is made by inventing homologous terms which slowly replace the "centers of interest" and the values postulated in the exchange of ideas. No, the illusion lies elsewhere, in the attempt to brake this movement, to think that it has become useless or dangerous, to want to fix one of these indispensable "passing phrases" and to take it by itself as *the* truth, when it is in fact no more than a *sign* or *symbol* of it. The error lies in refusing to allow others the right to be of some significance in the course of a period of evolution or tension, and in denying that there can be any reciprocity or any symbolism in these signs. By shutting itself up in its own witness, the experience contradicts what it claims to testify, namely "likeness" in "unlikeness", union in the midst of difference and a love that is always ready to move. The temptation is to accept fixation. Where God appears to be demanding revolutionary change, the devil always comes down on the side of the *status quo*.

In a thousand ways, illusion steals in to declare: "For myself —for us—*this* is what it means to be a Christian." The content of the "this" varies, but not the exclusiveness to which it lays claim. It may be the hermitage in the deserts of Egypt, or the epic companionship of a Crusade or a pilgrimage, or the blaze of light that comes to a soul in the course of psychological meditation, or the "good works" of active generosity, or even the sense of "committed" aroused by the consciousness of human responsibilities. In the course of the ages, each of these positions has had its corresponding and analogous movements in the culture of the period, and each of them has likewise had its spiritual obligations. But it ceases to be true, *even at the very heart and center of itself,* as soon as it does not look for some further stage—and this is always presaged by an element of encounter and contest, even if this only takes the modest but essential shape of one's relationships with a "spiritual father" and with one's brothers.

The truly "spiritual" person tends to receive as something significant the contradiction that comes to him from others or from events, and which is also revealed to him by the interior paradox of a *particular form* of faithfulness to *the Infinite*. And so negation becomes a form of "progress", and also the form assumed by their own "discourse", with the greatest of the mystics, such as Gregory of Nyssa, Master Eckhart or St. John of the Cross.[30] But an exactly contrary process—taking place, for instance, among their followers—blunts the edge of this unwearying boldness, and halts and fixes the negation at a particular stage, turning it into a spiritual "object", when it was meant to be a *movement*. Caught in the meshes of some group's "net", expressed in statue form or reduced to an ideology, the "letter" of a particular spiritual experience (with its psychological, sociological and mental determinants), no longer expresses what was its true spirit.

This paralysis is only too easy to understand; moreover, it explains the reactions that follow. It is discernable in the "spirituality" which petrifies the expression of this "rupture", necessary though it is, or in the "humanism" intoxicated by the sense that there is a something indispensable "to be added", although its meaning becomes progressively elusive. Only one element of the movement is retained, and then in a position of isolation which makes it no more than a caricature of the original. And this moment, taken out of its context, is no less revealing, for, like the photograph of a cross-section, it makes it possible to see the point at which *one* kind of spirituality takes root in the psychology and mental geography of a cosmic and social setting. For example, it cannot be denied that during the first half of the 17th century in France, the "invasion of the mystics" was closely

---

[30] J. Orcibal has analyzed the analogies between Master Eckhart and St. John of the Cross, and their common apophatism, in *Saint Jean de la Croix et les mystiques rhéno-flamands* (Paris, 1966), pp. 119-66.

bound up with the "Gentlemen of the Robe". Clearly, these "all-conquering" magistrates were then financing, supporting and filling the new institutes whose birth was heralded at the time with the trumpets of a new adventure on a level with the mystics' own. Clearly, there was a possible sociology here for the "spiritually-minded", and also a line of policy for them, and before long there was a "party" of the devout, confronting the progress of the centralizing power, devoid of all scruples about a dying Christianity and determined to turn the hierarchy of religion into a public service in the State.

The Judgment of Theology, Reason and Tradition

There is nothing surprising about this turn of events in the spiritual life, for this is the language that belongs to it. But spirituality becomes suspect when it no longer allows any opposition from those whom it confronts, when it becomes identified with the destinies of a particular group or policy, when the opposition "party" appears to be no longer capable of saying or revealing anything true *from its side, too,* in its own way about a fact which a particular "school" legitimately claims to assert from its own entrenched position. This reduction of the meaning to what seems significant, this restriction of the spirit to a "just that", is then used as a justification for a "reduction" in the opposite direction. Spiritual experience would then be considered by theologians as a purely "psychological phenomenon", by the philosophers as "sentimentalism" or "pragmatism", by the sociologist as the ideological defense of a particular group; by the historian as an extreme form taken by the culture of a particular period, etc. To be sure, these are all legitimate interpretations. And, more than this, they are indispensable for the full understanding of spiritual experience, for they prevent the identification of truth with any one of its expressions. At the present time, no less than in the past, the function they fulfill in the "spiritually minded" is one that has been continuously exercised by the demands, the "recalls" or the simple teachings of theology, reason or tradition.

Under these three different forms, the "rupture" reappears, but from this point it views the spiritual life as necessarily particular and private. Whether it be doctrinal, rational or historical, criticism puts what it has to say into a spiritual language. And this is an indispensable service, for it strips the vocabulary of "experiences" and "realities" of its mystical trappings and concentrates attention once again on its real meaning. Theological teaching is also bound up with a type of intelligibility and represents the objective side of revelation as a society founded on the recognition of one Spirit. The law of community which is "communion" (2 Cor. 13, 13) cannot fail to be of significance for those who testify and claim that by "new words" and present actions they are truly bearing witness to the work of the Holy Spirit in their day and age. In its own way, too, science (if we understand by this term the logic worked out in terms of the creative process expressed in its objects) should also rescue spiritual movements from the affective or subjective immediacy of an "experience" that is real enough, but not as yet at all clear as to its interior dialectic. It shatters a naive attachment to things by the very fact that it restores to the object or the experience its value as a sign (and an efficacious sign) in a "discourse" proportionate to what society thinks is "right". Finally, history reveals the cultural diversity of "spiritual" manifestations. The strangeness of the past confirms religious experience in its *movement,* but always with an element of surprise as it reveals, by showing the "differences" between the various periods, the spiritual meaning of each effort to get beyond the differences between contemporaries. And these are only three forms of finding the "other", which is the principle governing spiritual movement in modern culture.

V

CONCLUSION

The history of the religious vocabulary shows that the term *atheist* or *atheism* was used by the theologians against the "illuminati" or "spiritual" souls of the 16th century, and that Catholics and Protestants were soon using it mutually to describe one another. It was then reapplied to the Jansenists of the 18th century and the socialists of the 19th, etc. And inversely, the "atheists" used this word to define their reactions to the religion they saw in front of their eyes—a religion that believers coming one or two centuries later would have difficulty in recognizing as their own. On each occasion, the opposing parties enforced their reciprocal positions in absolute terms, when in truth they are relative and meant to be brought together. It is hard to see how things could be otherwise. Choices are always expressed in the precise terms supplied by a given culture, but although these terms are really relative, they look like the assumption of radical standpoints. Looking back on all this, we can learn a lesson. Just as the frontier between reason and unreason changes with the society of which it is the peculiar sign, so is the relationship between faith and atheism inseparable from the historical language that identifies it as a relationship between *this* faith and *this* atheism, or *these* believers and *their* adversaries.

The history of a word can teach a lesson, like a fable. There are two aspects of it which concern the problem of the relationships between spiritual movements and cultures. On the one hand, there is the relative nature of positions which can be defined in regard to one another in the cultural system of a particular time; on the other hand, there is the affirmation (at least in theory) of the identity between God and a specific position taken up by Christians, so that their opponents are classed as the opposition. The first aspect underlines the authenticity of the positions (whether they are "spiritual" or not) in a given mental outlook, and from this moment on there is a sense of "rupture" in the difference between the mental systems. The second aspect amounts to placing the real "rupture" at the point where any opposition is considered as tantamount to a refusal of God himself; for does not such intolerance in the face of any resistance and the refusal to admit that the other party may have any sense on their side block the way of faith? Moreover, such incapacity for understanding may appear in very different guises. It may take the form of an accusation of "atheism" leveled at an opponent, or what is very much the same thing—a contempt for the "devout". It may take the form of a self-sufficiency which refuses to admit the strange things that have happened in the past or the new situation created by the present, or it may appear as a rejection of any socio-cultural reading of spiritual experience, or a refusal to contemplate the possibility (and—as we should hold—the necessity) of reading the history of culture in a spiritual manner.

These two aspects allow us, in conclusion, to take up the question we started with in a somewhat different manner. On the one hand, we must recognize the validity of the positions which—although they may be called "spiritual" or "worldly", "supernatural" or "rational"—are not the less part and parcel of the culture of which they are both equally an expression. In this respect, their opponents or their critics are already bound up with the spiritual movements that react against them or stand out in distinction from them. They are tied to one another by a cultural solidarity, not only in spite of, but actually because of, their very differences.

But the Christian must recognize a meaning in this situation with which he is in fact confronted, for it marks out for him a task, a task to be faced today, and one for which he can be grateful. Through his efforts to live out as a faithful Christian the nameless demands that his own inventions make upon man, he discovers hitherto unperceived elements in his own faith and the existing expression of his response to God. The ecumenical movement opens up for him the untroubled freedom that orthodoxy has preserved in its attitude to the holy mysteries, or an understanding of scripture for which Protestant devotion and exegesis have prepared the way. The social movements of today show him how to read the Gospel of Nazareth with contemporary understanding. The scientific discoveries teach him the full dimensions of Genesis and of man's responsibilities which his faith had already taught him, but only in terms of a past culture.

The study of the development of law gives him a better appreciation of God's respect for freedom of conscience. What comes to him through television shows him the imagery that expresses the urgency of a universal Christian solidarity. All these are new discoveries which God in his mercy has allowed to come about, and by the grace of God they must be used in approaching him in the language of today; for it must not be forgotten that only through this new cultural conditioning[31] is there the possibility of deepening our spiritual experiences in all these ways.

[31] Cf. M. de Certeau, "Situations culturelles, vocation spirituelle," in *Christus* 43 (1964), pp. 294-313; "Expérience chrétienne et langages de la foi," in *Christus* 46 (1965), pp. 147-63.

Bernard Cooke, S.J./*Milwaukee, Wis.*

Existential Pertinence
of Religion

In all parts of the world today religion is faced with the charge of irrelevance, and Christianity is not exempt from this charge. Nietzsche's phrase, "God is dead", finds a resonance in many quarters: in contemporary literature, in the theater, even in art, and the phrase is being bandied about among those who have suddenly become enamored of the "God is dead" theology. Much contemporary psychology looks upon religion as a source of human retardation, a refuge which deprives people of the determination and forthrightness they require in order to solve their psychological problems, an imposition of fear and domination in the psychological life of man that stands as a barrier to his true, free development. And in the large portions of the world where a view of life flowing from Marxist theology is dominant, the judgment that "religion is the opium of the people" finds expression in official policies and to quite an extent apparently in the lives of people.

Nor are the charges of irrelevance totally unfounded. In the modern world the burden of proof rests upon believers to show that the forms of religious expression and the patterns of religious activity really have an existential importance for the development of man, both in his individual life and in his societal existence. This, then, is the question to which the present article addresses itself: Can one find patterns of thinking, patterns of basic attitude, patterns of behavior which are proper to Christianity and which make it possible for man to be more profoundly human, to exist with purpose and meaning beyond what could be reached apart from Christianity?

I

VISION OF LIFE

Basic to any culture is a view of life. This would be most essentially an anthropology, but an anthropology polarized both by a cosmology and by a theology, a vision of man that takes into account the fact that man is a being in the world and that man somehow rises above this world and points by his very personal way of being to some transcendent destiny with God. It is a truism in the history of Western thought that man's culture and man's thought-world are dominated by the way in which man thinks of the three great areas of reality: world, self and God. Beneath this truism lies the fact that man's personal existence in any given period of history is radically controlled by the vision he possesses of the reality or unreality, the importance or unimportance, of one or other of these basic realities.

In this regard Christianity has a unique perspective to communicate to man, a unique and paradoxical insight into the structure of human existence and human meaning. The basic truth of Christianity, around which everything else turns, is the mystery of the death and resurrection of Christ. This is the Gospel; this is the first kerygma that formed the Christian community itself, and on the basis of which it approached the world and strove to convert it to Christianity.

A person or a culture can think of man as polarized only by the negating fact of death. In this case the world is a riddle, man himself an enigma and God a totally unknown. But the revelation of Christianity consists in the fact that death is not the final reference for man, but rather the penultimate reality, a threshold for that which alone is the final stage of human existing: resurrection.[1] The resurrection of Christ, in which man is meant to participate, gives to the course of human history and to the evolution of the cosmos a personally eschatological dimension.

Mankind is a people on the march toward fulfillment. The world participates in this to the extent that man will utilize this world in the context of his own thrust toward fulfillment and complete its intelligibility by inserting into it his own creative ideas. God is not a totally unknown being, standing apart from human history and the world of creation. He is involved in the very processes of human history because of the mystery of incarnation. The eschatology that guides the teleological evolution of created reality (including man) is an eschatology not only rooted in, but actually identified with, the risen Christ. He, the *eschaton,* in his own individual human existence, stands in the final stage of human history. But he remains present to the Christian community and through it to all mankind. Through his redemptive love he gradually assimilates the human race to that state of personal fulfillment which represents the destiny of man individually and societally.

II

CHRISTIAN SELF-IDENTITY

Again, one can point to the way in which the Christian perspective—human life clarified by the mystery of Christ's death and resurrection—provides a new and more radical principle of self-identity. Such self-identification is, of course, of critical importance in the existential situation of man, individually and socially. Unless a man can determine who he is, not only by way of discovery but also by way of self-creativity, he can never attain to personal fulfillment; life is a meaningless situation in

[1] Besides Durrwell's book, *The Resurrection* (New York, 1960), two other studies on the resurrection might be noted: D. Stanley, *Christ's Resurrection in Pauline Soteriology* (Rome, 1961), and W. Künneth, *The Theology of the Resurrection* (London, 1965).

which one remains a mystery to himself. Unless a society can establish some identification, it is unable to provide an intelligible context for the development of the individuals who make up that society.

Christianity, with its teaching about the continuing presence of the risen Christ to the Christian community and with its sacramental celebration of the passover of Christ wherein Christians can experientially come in contact with this risen Christ, does provide a new ground of identification.[2] The Christian is who he is because God incarnate is actually identified with him by the mystery of becoming man, and because he thus can come into human identification with this person Jesus who himself is God. The continuing presence of Christ in the Church through sacrament makes it possible for the Christian, beginning with baptism and continuing through the whole context of the sacramental life, to find conscious identification with Christ.

To be a Christian means much more than to bear an empty title or the responsibility for fulfilling certain religious rituals. To be a Christian means to stand in profound identification with this man who is Jesus of Nazareth, passed now into fulfillment of life and remaining with us so that we also might find such fullness. Not only does one find identification with this individual who is Christ, but in terms of that identification one finds community identity with all others who share faith in the mystery of the risen Christ. This self-identification extends in the mystery of grace to the Father, who is the Father of Jesus Christ but who is also, for those who are identified with Christ, their Father. Man has identification, then, not just in terms of the constantly changing processes of human history and human relationship, but in the ultimate and unchanging context of the three divine Persons offering themselves to man in profound personal friendship.

The self-identification that Christians have in community can be seen in functional terms: their baptism gives them an orientation to an historical function which is that of entering into the

[2] Cf. *Constitution on the Sacred Liturgy*, nn. 6-7.

redemption of mankind.[3] The People of God, the Christian community, is a priestly people, charged with fulfilling at a given
point in history the priestly and redemptive mission of Christ
himself. Thus the very experience of participation in Christian
life and the Christian apostolate should give, not just to the individual Christian but to Christians in community, a sense of
achievement, a sense of purpose and a location in the processes
of mankind's developing history.

It is one of the characteristics of modern life that we search
for historical understandings. We are intrigued by the evolutionary dimension of reality and we try to explain ourselves in
terms of our antecedents. Christianity is totally compatible with
this cast of mind, because among the religions of mankind it is
characterized by its historical perspective. If one accepts the
realities communicated to one in Christian faith, history assumes
an intelligible pattern in the midst of which one can locate
oneself.[4] The life of man on this planet is not simply a meaningless progression toward no one knows what goal. Human
history is a working out of the design of God that focuses on
the mystery of Christ and the extension of his influence in the
life of mankind.

The individual Christian in the Church at any point in its
history can realize that this is the latest stage in the development
of the mystery of Christ, a stage that must itself give way to
future generations of Christians as they express in even fuller
form the developing mystery of man's salvation in Christ. Thus,
for an individual Christian, life is full of meaning because of his
relationship to Christ and his relationship to others in the mystery of the Church, past, present and yet to come. He can find
identification as one united to Christ and one in whom the mystery of Christ is expressed in unrepeatable fashion. He can find
identification as a son of God the Father, related to this Person

[3] Cf. *Constitution on the Church*, n. 34.
[4] An excellent summary of current Christian thinking on the meaning
of history is given by J. Connolly, *Human History and the Word of God*
(New York, 1965).

who is the ultimate destiny, just as he is the ultimate source, of all reality.

In terms of the vision of life, which is required in order that man's existence have concrete pertinence, Christianity would seem to have something invaluable to offer, not just as interior faith, but in its external forms—its liturgy, its catechesis, its societal existence. It provides man with a view of life that makes it possible for him to exist with meaning, with understanding and with psychological security. And to the extent that an individual Christian or a group of Christians are more fully formed to such understandings and exposed to meaningful experiences of Christian life, they will be enabled to be more fully human and to express in the rest of their living the depths of personality with which they have been endowed.

III

AFFECTIVE OPENNESS

However, human life and human personality are not just a matter of cognition. We are becoming more and more aware in the modern world that to be a person means to be open in relatedness to other persons. This applies both to individuals and to human society.[5] One of the gravest problems confronting us at the present time is the separation of man from man, the alienation of peoples one from another, the anonymity that is developing amidst the complexities of our contemporary civilization.[6] Accompanying this are increasing fears that assail man because of the threats that surround him, and these in turn tend to close off man from man.

In the midst of this, religion—particularly institutionalized

[5] Cf. E. Fromm, *The Act of Loving* (New York, 1956), and *The Sane Society* (London, 1956).

[6] Cf. H. Cox, *The Secular City* (New York, 1965), pp. 38-59; D. Riesman, *The Lonely Crowd* (New York, 1953); P. Tillich, *The Courage To Be* (New York, 1952).

religion—does not seem to be any great help. As a matter of
fact, the institutionalized religious expressions of Western Europe and America seem to provide one of the greatest bar-
riers to human unification. We are faced with antagonisms
and oppositions despite the advance of the ecumenical movement in our own day. Many people are seriously asking: "Would
we not be better off as a human race if there were no institutionalized forms of religion to which men were committed, so
that men could simply approach God on a basis of their own
inner faith and on the basis of their generous devotion to one
another?" However, it would seem that this is a shallow and
inadequate answer to the problem in its real dimensions.

What Christianity tells us is that man is most fully man, truly
open to human communication and personal development, because of the mystery of the presence of God. Human beings
develop as humans, open to the mystery of human friendship and
love and intercommunication, because of the impact of the presence of persons in their experience. But the greatest persons that
come into the range of understanding of the Christian are the
Father, the Son and the Holy Spirit. Their presence, their being
not only with us but for us, is what is meant to shatter the psychological substructures of the human person and of human
society and to open them up to a whole new range of personal
existence.

This openness of man to personal existence by the loving
presence of God is not something that takes place in utter hid-
denness. It is meant to function in and through the consciousness
that man has of this mystery of divine presence. To put it in
other words, the self-giving of God to man is conditioned by
man's acceptance of this presence of faith. The Word of God,
which is a life-giving force, can give life only in proportion as
man is willing to hear this Word.

Thus the full impact of the transforming presence of God
requires an accurate consciousness of this presence on the part
of Christians. But if such consciousness is to be accurate, there
must be in Christian society some institutionalized criteria that

can be the norm of guiding man's appraisal of this divine presence. Only in this way will one's understanding be accurate and not totally dependent upon subjective inclinations. Moreover, if man is to experience God together in community, it would seem that situations must be provided that make it possible for such experience to take place. And while one does not limit the experience of God in faith to the verbally formulated criteria for faith or limit this experience to the moments of structured liturgical action, nevertheless, the history of the past few centuries indicates quite clearly that the question of faith criteria is of major importance in the life of man.[7]

IV

EXPERIENCE OF COMMUNITY

Another element, which is critical in Christianity's contribution to man, is the experience of sharing community. This experience is most centrally that of liturgical action, but it is not limited to this. It extends to all the areas of human life in which Christians can share a common purpose and a common concern. However, for this experience to be really vital and transformative of the individual and of society, it must be a conscious experience and an educated experience. Only the conscious confrontation with the mystery of Christ constitutes the true context of faith and makes it possible for a Christian community to see its world and its own history in the light of the mystery of the risen Christ.[8] Again, if such accurate understanding and such intelligent and meaningful experience are to take place, there must be a development of the affectivity, cognition and decisiveness of a given group of Christians.

This would seem to require forms of religious expression, structures of religious life, the institutionalization of the com-

---

[7] This lies at the root of the present hermeneutical discussions. Cf. the series *New Frontiers in Theology*, ed. J. Robinson and J. Cobb (New York, 1963ff.).

[8] Cf. *Constitution on the Sacred Liturgy*, nn. 10, 47-48.

munity's Christian being. Obviously there must be flexibility in this. The institutional aspects of Christian religious life must always be open to the mystery of conversion and reform. But to say this in no way denies the necessity of having forms of external expression and activity that are so radically important in shaping the inner consciousness and attitudes of human beings.

Psychology has made a major contribution to modern man's self-awareness. Because of its insights, individual men and whole societies are better able to understand their motivations, attitudes and activity. At the same time this increased awareness of man's inner life has at times led to a preoccupation with man's psychological needs and an unhealthy self-centeredness. Many of the young, in particular, seem to become obsessed by the objectives of self-fulfillment and do not adequately enough realize that this fulfillment can only come in selflessness and self-giving. It is critical that the mystery of Christian self-giving operate in a society to keep it from becoming narcissistically introverted. To establish a stable context of Christian experience of genuine love is one of the most radically important contributions that Christians should make to human life at the present time. Only when the dignity of the human person and his transcendent ultimacy are experienced in terms of profound interpersonal love will we have a vision of man that can stand as a norm of judging the complex societal and technological transformations occurring in our day. Only if such a profound vision of man is operative can we safeguard the dignity of man and keep him from being absorbed into processes that would depersonalize him.

V

STRUGGLE AGAINST EVIL

Christian revelation tells us that the experience of man is a complex affair involving a dialectic between the forces of good and evil. Non-Christian experience cannot tell us directly about the mystery of sin, man's involvement in it and his redemption from it. Yet the experience of mankind does attest to a certain tension within human experience between the elements of order and the elements of chaos. Ancient peoples were aware of this tension and tried to provide for its resolution in religious myths and rituals. Old Testament and New Testament revelation has situated the root of this difficulty in man's abuse of his own freedom, and it has recognized that from this abuse of freedom have resulted those intricate patterns of disorder and unruly activity that have characterized the up-and-down career of mankind over the centuries. There is a mystery of evil that exists not only in the consciousness and deliberation of man, but is found in every situation of human existence and is translated into those patterns of life that have worked to restrict, dominate and even destroy the human person.[9] One need go no further back into history than the disastrous results of Nazism to see the way in which the mystery of evil has found expression in the patterned existence of mankind.

Against this mystery of evil, man finds himself pitted by his own purposeful self-position. If the root of the problem of evil lies in man's abuse of this freedom, then the resolution of this problem must lie somewhere in the area of man's authentic use of the freedom and responsibility that are his. This has been the dominant theme in the currents of thought associated with personalism and existentialism in the 20th century. Christianity promises a deepening to this insight, a context of understanding with regard to freedom and responsibility and self-position which can give, if not an adequate answer, at least a context of human life that eschatologically points toward the fulfillment of man in this very dimension of his being. Somehow in the career of mankind there must eventuate an assertion of man in free responsibility or the destiny of man can never be fulfilled.

Christian formation, if it be faithful to itself, is essentially a formation toward responsible freedom. The entire progression of revelation, both in the Old and New Testaments, is a movement

[9] Cf. P. Schoonenberg, *Sin and Man* (Notre Dame, 1965), particularly his chapter on "The Sin of the World".

in the direction of the increased freedom of the individual and of man living in society. Such freedom can be attained only if the individuals who form that society come to an understanding of their own identity and know their purpose in the historical process. Nor is this formation one that can be attained simply by academic instruction. It requires such instruction either formally or informally, plus the deepening that comes through liturgical experience and involvement in the responsible life of the community. Thus the development of religious culture is a basic requirement in attaining Christianity's goal for the individual person and for human society. Without such formation, Christianity (in its human elements) remains very largely a superficial reality, witnessing neither to itself nor to the presence of God in the world.

The freedom that Christians are meant to possess involves freedom from those fears that inhibit individuals and societies, that keep them from being true to themselves and that prevent their achieving the goals for which they exist.[10] Christian redemption is meant to be redemption from just such fears, a redemption that is effected by psychological security that comes through divine and human acceptance and through the identification that one discovers in religious community. Such freedom from fear, such orientation toward free decision, demands for its own stability the solidity of established community structures upon which one can depend, and in terms by which one can find a frame of reference for his thought and his activity.

Thus in the attainment of personal freedom, the formalized and institutionalized aspects of Christianity seem to be of great importance. Granted, again, that these may oftentimes fail to achieve their purpose because they are overly systematized or too rigid, the answer does not lie in the abolition of such institutional forms, but in their establishment in fidelity to their own genius and the nature of the truth they are meant to bear.

However, the social dynamics of the Christian community

[10] Cf. C. Rogers, *On Becoming a Person* (Boston, 1961), pp. 39-58, 103-25.

are not self-centered. The People of God does not exist for itself, but in order to bear witness to the redeeming presence of Christ that is intended to transform the entire context of human living. Therefore, the faith of Christians in its expression in institutionalized forms has a pertinence that extends to all mankind in each period of human history. Christian life bears the inescapable imperative that Christians better the social situation in which they find themselves.[11] Thus, it provides for Christians an authentic and altruistic context for the expression of their aggressive impulses. Christians are meant to find their self-fulfillment in the area of achievement, not through self-centered and selfish endeavor, but through the application of their powers of achievement to the betterment of the entire situation of mankind. If it be true to its own nature, the Christian community is as profoundly humanistic in its orientation as is any other grouping of human beings—indeed, more so, because it professes to see for mankind an ultimacy and a dignity and a hope for achievement beyond anything that man can grasp apart from the insight of faith.

Man is meant to live in society. He is meant to establish for himself that pattern of human experience, insight and achievement that we call human culture. Of this continuing endeavor, the evolution and betterment of the human condition, the Christian is meant to be an integral part. His Christianity is meant not to divorce him from the life of men, but to immerse him in it by way of identification and transformation. By so doing, the Christian will witness to the fact that religion, rather than being a principle of retardation, is a dynamic influence for the betterment of mankind. Rather than God being dead, a genuine understanding of God manifested in the mystery of the risen Christ can be a transforming influence for the betterment of human life.

[11] *Pastoral Constitution on the Church in the Modern World,* nn. 25-39.

Robert Bultot / *Louvain, Belgium*

The Theology of Earthly Realities and Lay Spirituality

Any Christian spirituality depends on moral and dogmatic theology. A lay spirituality therefore presupposes a theology of the lay state. One can approach this from two points of view: one can start from a general ecclesiology—the natural inclination of the clerical theologian—or one can start from the lay condition itself as, I think, most laymen do with equal naturalness when they begin to think of themselves in theological terms. Whichever view one takes, the very nature of the layman is bound to lead to, and to answer, one of the most fundamental questions of ecclesiology. More radically still, it forces us to take a new look at the very *subject* of theology, for "the subject of theology is the living God. Insofar as created beings are concerned, this discipline deals with them inasmuch as they are related to this living God as to their principle or their end".[1]

The Christian layman is by definition a man who takes upon himself in a singular fashion the fullness of the human condition in both its natural and supernatural dimensions. This implies, therefore, the whole question of the relations between creation and redemption in all its radicalness. One cannot fit it into ecclesiology without reference to its concrete nature, and this

[1] Y. Congar, *La foi et la théologie* (Tournai, 1962), p. 133.

44

requires a theology of the realities of this earth.[2] Moreover, this problem shows that the layman constitutes the very link between the Church and the world and that, in the mission of the Church, he plays a part peculiarly his own, not in the least an auxiliary part but an essential one.

Historically speaking, it is significant that the emancipation of the laity goes hand in hand with the autonomy (not the same as independence) of secular reality. The Church has had to become more aware of this reality. From the lay point of view there are here two aspects of a single statement, namely that creation, of which the laity have an immediate experience as men and women, has a consistency of its own, a meaning of its own and a specific value; from the lay point of view, furthermore, there are two aspects of a single question, which is that of the concrete relationship between secular history and salvation history, and this question is proposed by the laity as Christians to the Church as a divine institution.

When we examine the past with a mind as acutely aware of nature as of grace, we see without any doubt that the state of remote inferiority in which the laity were kept for so long in the Church was largely due[3] to that certain lack of recognition of secular values and even that disparagement of various aspects of man's earthly condition that one can find among religious people, theologians and pastors throughout the centuries. The layman appeared as a second-class Christian because the Church as an institution was so slow in accepting the specific meaning of creation—that is, not the directly symbolical or religious meaning.

Undoubtedly, there have always been within Christianity vari-

[2] "A complete theology of the laity would be a complete ecclesiology; it would also be an anthropology and even a theology of creation in its relation to christology" (Y. Congar, *Jalons pour une théologie du laïcat* [Paris, 1953], p. 14; Eng. tr. *Lay People in the Church* [Westminster, Md.: Newman Press, 1965]).

[3] More than it was due to the various encroachments of the "secular" power; see R. Cox, *A Study of the Juridic Status of Laymen in the Writing of the Medieval Canonists* (Washington, 1959). Nor was it due so much to the reaction against heretical anti-hierarchical movements.

ous currents that were more or less favorable to the natural reality. Nevertheless, the attitudes of distrust and even hostility were sufficiently predominant, in spite of some truly humanist tendencies, to create, little by little, a divorce between Christianity and modern society since the Renaissance.

Several factors contributed to this phenomenon. First of all, we must admit that sometimes the religious spirit was colored by a certain "imperialism" which required *a priori* the maximum for God and the minimum for man, going so far as to reduce man to as little as possible, whether in matters concerning grace and freedom or in any other problem. Moreover, the bible was not meant to provide us with scientific knowledge but only to reveal the supernatural plan of God, and it insists rather one-sidedly on God's transcendence and omnipotence, sometimes at the expense of secondary causes, so that its partial character and particular orientation have brought about a certain imbalance and prevented Christians for a long time from being as open to the meaning of creation as they ought to be. For example, the word "world" is never used in New Testament writings in the passages that speak of the kingship and lordship of Christ over the universe; instead, the words "all" and "all things" are used as in the Hebrew. On the other hand, this word "world" appears very often in a morally and religiously pejorative sense that does not agree with the cosmological and sociological sense. This use of the term "world" was apt to damage the true view of the earthly condition.

Before the positive and ultimate message of the bible could become clear with regard to the realities of this earth,[4] it needed a set of historical circumstances that were not immediately present. The hostility of the Roman Empire toward the first Christians and the idolatrous and immoral character of the society in which they found themselves, contributed largely to value judgments that prevented them from seeing the earthly city in its true nature as the work of man. After that, the political, administrative, economic and cultural structures of the Empire

[4] Cf. M. Dubarle, *Optimisme devant ce monde* (Paris, 1949).

collapsed and created a void. The Church, which in the mean-time had acquired a privileged and already dominant position since Constantine, filled that void by taking the place of the civil powers and assuming functions that did not derive from its mis-sion. Thus there arose a Christian "regime." This consisted in a general clericalization of activities which derived their meaning and justification only because they were put to immediate use for supernatural or ecclesiastical ends. Thus the natural order found itself in some way deprived of its proper character and intrinsic meaning to the advantage of a purely religious meaning. It was confiscated and absorbed before it ever had a chance to be itself.

On the other hand, ideas of Greek origin infiltrated very early the concept that many Christian authors built up for them-selves about man and his world. Without doubt, the formal heresies of Origen and his disciples were condemned by the Councils of that time. But several of their ideas, to which the authority paid less attention or showed itself more amenable because they were anthropological rather than christological, continued to circulate anonymously and to be handed down *incognito* through the course of the centuries. In Clement, Origen, Methodius of Olympus, Athanasius, Basil, Gregory of Nazianzen, Gregory of Nyssa, Ambrose and Augustine the pejorative Greek notions about the body and the flesh, based on a metaphysical dualism, coexisted contradictorily with the moral and unitary notions of the bible. This affected their representation of the human condition and, of course, their spirituality.

Within this heterogeneous context Paul's conflict between the "flesh" and the "spirit" was often interpreted on the lines of Platonist categories.[5] In Evagrius of Pontus, the main represen-tative of that Origenism which was condemned in 553 by the Fifth Council of Constantinople, the ascetical and mystical teach-ing is so closely tied up with his metaphysics, anthropology and cosmology that one can only understand it as part of the whole

[5] See P. Daubercies, *La condition charnelle. Recherches positives pour la théologie d'une réalité terrestre* (Tournai, 1959).

system: "Only there does it show its true nature and its true meaning. . . . On the other hand, his metaphysics cannot be severed from his ascetical and mystical teaching which is its concrete and practical application." [6]

Evagrius taught a theory of a twofold creation: the creation of invisible beings, pure intellects at first, whose activity was exhausted in the knowledge of God; they neglectfully turned away from him and in consequence of this "fall" God created the visible world, adjusted to their downfall, so that they might, thanks to the substitute of sense-knowledge, gradually return to their first condition. His eschatology leads to a complete and final disappearance of the body. His asceticism is conceived in terms of this origin and this return: the presence of man in a body and in a material universe is seen as the result of the fall, an exile with which one has to bear impatiently in the hope of being delivered from it; one must try as much as possible to get rid of the hold that matter has on us. The Greeks and Syrians tried artificially to detach Evagrius' ascetical and mystical teaching from its natural framework so that it could be used by orthodox monks. But this expurgation was far from complete. As much as one would like to cut his most explicit heterodox theses out of such a coherent system of thought, in some subtle way the structure of the whole keeps on appearing in what is left of it; the spirit that inspires the whole continues to permeate from within.

John Cassian, who had such a profound influence on the monastic tradition of the West, stands between East and West. But Cassian was a disciple of Evagrius and his ascetical teaching depends essentially on the practice of his master. Hence the formidable problem with which historians of spirituality have been confronted for some years: "How far has the Origenism of Evagrius conditioned the spirituality of hesychasm (to arrive through ascetic practices at the perfect 'quiet'—*hesuchos*—of body and mind to achieve the vision of God) and the ascetic

---

[6] A. Guillaumont, Les *"Kephalia gnostica"* d'Evagre le Pontique et *l'histoire de l'orgénisme chez les Grecs et chez les Syriens* (Paris, 1962; Patrist. Sorbon. 5), p. 336.

tradition of the West?"[7] The teaching of the double creation runs more or less explicitly throughout the early Middle Ages and one finds it in St. Gregory the Great, in Odo of Cluny who copies him, and in John Scotus Erigena.[8]

The first great theological developments took place in the cultural milieu of Hellenism where the philosophers, very different in this from the inspired authors, had practically no historical sense at all. For the Greeks "to become" meant to change, to degrade oneself; it was an evil. However much he was a theologian of history, St. Augustine saw time as a result of sin, an environment that was alien to man and where he found himself in exile.[9] For him time produces nothing by itself; on the contrary, it dissolves all; anything that is positive in history comes from divine grace. The famous comparison of the People of God with a man who grows up (*De vera relig.*, 50; *In Ps. 118*, 16, 6; *De Civ. Dei* X, 14) only concerns the religious aspect. Moreover, since according to Genesis God rested on the seventh day, some saw in this "sabbath" the ceasing of all movement, of all "becoming" in creation: creation was finished and done with. Sin appeared as a radically new event on the fringe, and this was the beginning of history, but it was to be a history of *souls,* based on a creation that was finished once and for all. The world was reduced to a mere theatrical setting with regard to the temporal drama of salvation which now stood in the foreground. Salvation, understood as the whole of God's efforts and those of the believer to overcome evil, was no longer lived out as a progressive realization of a fullness of meaning and an increase in "being",

[7] Fr. Refoulé, "La mystique d'Evagre et l'Origénisme," in *Vie spir.* 66 (Sept. 1963), pp. 461-2.

[8] Gregory the Great, *Moralia in Job*, V, 61 (*P.L.* 75, 712D-713A); Odo of Cluny, *Collationes,* III, 29 (*P.L.* 133, 612A-D); for John Scotus Erigena, cf. M. Cappuyns, *Jean Scot Erigène. Sa vie, son oeuvre, sa pensée* (Louvain/Paris, 1933, pp. 357-8, 370, 373-4; E. Gilson, *La philosophie au moyen âge* (Paris,³1948), p. 218 (tr.: New York, 1955).

[9] St. Augustine, *In Epist. Joh. ad Parth.,* 11, 10; *In Ps. 147,* 5; *In Ps. 146,* 4; cf. Plotinus, *Ennéades* (ed. Bréhier), III, 7 and X, 7. Cf. L. Boros, "Les catégories de la temporalité chez saint Augustin," in *Arch. de philos.* 22 (1958), pp. 323-85.

no longer as a positive achievement, but as a *rescue operation* from a creation that had become dangerous. It was interpreted wrongly as an end in itself, distinct from the end of creation, which had become irrelevant. All along the line the problems of evil and salvation became detached from that of creation.[10]

A careful examination of numerous patristic and medieval texts thus indicates the kind of anthropology they contain. It was a philosophy of man and the world, undoubtedly neither systematic nor technical, but on the contrary expressed in the simple language of ordinary life, and yet on occasion astonishingly coherent, two qualities that ensured a profound grip on the contemporary mind. On the whole it produced the idea that in the beginning man was a spiritual or spiritualized being, alien to sex, world and secular activities, vowed solely to a contemplation of God placing him beyond the influence of time.

Thus, the earthly condition and the activities linked with it were devalued, and how could the lay state, which is precisely defined in these terms, escape from the same devaluation? World and worldly, time and temporal (*siècle* and *séculier*)—words that could have and sometimes did have a positive or at least a neutral sense, and sometimes a negative sense from the moral and religious point of view—frequently had both meanings at the same time. In many texts "secular" refers to the layman who lives *in* the *saeculum* in the double sense of profane society and corrupt society; he lives there according to the "world" also in a double sense, according to the specific aspects of the earthly condition (marriage, job, property, etc.) and in a spirit of immorality and irreligion. "To leave the world" meant at the same time to leave the lay way of life and the so-called life of sin. The laity were presented as *carnal* as opposed to the monks and clergy who were *spiritual,* and this not even in an exclusively Pauline sense but in a sense colored by the metaphysical aspects of an anthropology outlined above.[11]

[10] Cf. P. Ricoeur, *Philosophie de la volonté. II, Finitude et culpabilité. 2, La symbolique du mal* (Paris, 1960), pp. 163-4 (tr. in preparation).

[11] For a further and more developed analysis in a particular case, see R. Bultot, *La doctrine du mépris du monde* . . . , vol. I: *Pierre Damien* (Louvain/Paris, 1963), pp. 17-65.

This then was the context within which the teaching of the contempt of the world developed and flourished.[12] This expression did not have only one meaning: sometimes this *contempt of the world* referred to the simple rejection of sin and the refusal to regard the goods of this earth as the supreme values of life, which might apply to all Christians; at other times it referred to a monastic renunciation of a certain number of goods and legitimate activities. But if it is not always the case, it nevertheless often happens that these two forms of contempt of the world go hand in hand with a genuine disparagement of the realities which are renounced and detachment from which is extolled. A whole list of contrasts insinuates this devaluation of the world: *changing-stable, transient-eternal, earthly-heavenly, carnal-spiritual, senses-intelligence, visible-invisible, etc.* Paralyzed by contingencies, it has no value except as a heap of moral and religious symbols that can be molded at random by divine initiative. All these contrasts do not merely reflect the lack of a common measure between creator and creature and the lack of proportion between the infinite and the finite. In many cases the more or less Platonist anthropology mentioned above can be felt underneath these value judgments giving them a philosophical perspective. In any case, this one-sided attention paid to the contingency and finiteness of created beings, which appear so radical when confronted with the divine Absolute, does not represent their full value. To know them as they are (after having seen what they are not) and to appreciate them objectively, one has to examine their concrete nature and their own distinctive existence.[13] In short, this contempt of the world may be a wholesome reminder to man that he transcends the universe, that he is called to a life of another order, a supernatural one, and that he alienates himself if he limits his ambitions exclusively to what is of this earth; it may be the genuine expression of a preference for God, either through detachment and a certain basic aloofness toward all that is created or through the renouncement of certain human goods.

---

[12] For its history, see my other works.

[13] Cf. C. Duquoc, "Eschatologie et réalités terrestres," in *Lum. et vie* 9 (1960), n. 50, pp. 13-14.

Nevertheless, this contempt of the world, *as it stands revealed in history,* does not always do justice to those earthly realities or to the works of man.

A Hellenistic legacy that devalued the carnal condition, man's presence in a material universe, the active life, time and sex; a debatable exegesis that provided certain theories with a semblance of biblical foundation but which in reality projected *a priori* some preconceived notions derived from a particular historical mentality; the collapse of the structures of a bygone society and the decline of a secular civilization—all these factors jeopardized the authentic love of God and the application of certain evangelical values because of a view of man and the world that cast a bad light on even the characteristic features of the lay way of life. This went so far that such a way of life was not only seen as less perfect but "almost as a life of no-grace",[14] while the specific features of it were seen as obstacles to salvation.[15]

It is not in the nature of things for civil society to remain in a permanent state of collapse or for secular activities to remain in a state of permanent atrophy with their purpose blurred or even unnoticed. Gradually, from the time of the Middle Ages, the order of secular realities reasserted itself in a normal way; man's conscience became again aware of them, and the need for a certain felt, legitimate autonomy arose.[16] Those who were responsible for the Church were wrong in jamming their theology with a presentation of man and the universe that had had its time[17] and to cling to a political-religious system they presumptu-

---

[14] G. Miccoli, "Théologie de la vie monastique chez St. Pierre Damien," in *Théologie de la vie monastique* (Paris, 1961), p. 47.

[15] I have only mentioned the more negative current of thought for the reason explained at the beginning. But there was at the same time, in a measure that varied according to the age, a more positive attitude, assessing the classes and functions of society, with a theory about the *ordines,* sermons on the state of life, etc.

[16] See, for instance, G. de Lagarde, *La naissance de l'esprit laïc au déclin du moyen âge* (Louvain/Paris, 1956-1963), five vols.

[17] See R. Lavocat, *L'Eglise et la Communauté scientifique internationale* (Paris, 1965).

ously considered adequate and final. There was a great lack of reflection in that "violent" synthesis of the Christian "regime".[18] This lack of reflection was partly inevitable, for religious awareness must mature with time; it cannot immediately see all the truths it is capable of seeing; it must discover them with the help of reason enlightened by grace and assisted by the progress of secular history itself. But this lack of reflection was also partly due to a "totalitarian" religious impulse, in the sense that some people decide *a priori* that to recognize any value at all in man, except evil, is to take away something from God.

Insofar as this theological synthesis was prematurely concluded and became fixed, it forced any movement toward a legitimate recovery of the secular, any claim made in favor of the values of the worldly element, to assert itself *against* the "Church" and necessarily to take on the semblance of an apostasy. The result was the divorce now existing between Christianity and the modern world. As man extended and deepened his investigation of the universe, particularly since the Renaissance, and as he investigated his own condition, he discovered with the strong certainty of immediate evidence that he held a real power of mastery and transformation over nature; he discovered that, far from being an exile in a universe alien to his soul, this universe was his natural environment, and even his matrix. For he humanized himself and became more specifically himself only by remolding the universe according to his needs, his ambitions and his dreams. The unfolding of the sciences, technology, economics, politics and arts in a social development on the crest of a cosmic development—that is the truly human way to exist.

However, the Church did not keep the same pace. In the past it had often distrusted innovations and discoveries; it suspected progress, and it sometimes rooted up the wheat with the weeds.[19] Decidedly, Christianity seemed to know precious little about man, and still less about how to encourage him; this became the

[18] On this notion of violence, see P. Ricoeur, *Histoire et vérité* (Paris, 1955), pp. 141-82. (tr.: Evanston, 1965).

[19] Cf. C. Duquoc, *L'Eglise et le progrès* (Paris, 1964).

drama of atheistic humanism[20] and, within the Church, the great grief of the most enlightened laity.

In his analysis of historical consciousness Pierre-Henri Simon observed in 1954: "The condemnation of the modern world, frequent and often violent among Christians, is not merely inspired by an upsurge of repugnance with regard to a materialistic civilization that has been voided of God; more generally it hides a permanent tendency to emphasize the separation of the two cities, the two kinds of history. If the modern world appears as the adversary that must be overcome and the evil spirit that must be exorcised, this is not so much because of its exceptional maliciousness as because it incarnates the secular world *here and now,* and this secular world is condemned." [21]

The voice of revolt was raised against this unjust condemnation: "My most intimate and most unshakable conviction—too bad for orthodoxy if it is heretical—is that, whatever so many spiritual and learned men may have said, God does in no way want to be loved by us in opposition to the creature, but he wants to be glorified through the creature and starting from the creature. That is why I cannot bear so many spiritual writings. That God, who is set up against all that is created and who is in some way jealous of his own handiwork, is but an idol in my eyes. It is a relief for me to have written this. And I declare that until I retract this I shall be insincere whenever I seem to state anything contrary to what I have just written." These tragic words were written by Gabriel Marcel in his *Journal métaphysique,* dated March 5, 1933.

Thus, both from outside and from inside the Church, the voice of creation was heard, more or less clearly, by the theologians and pastors whose attention had until then been too exclusively occupied with sin and its consequences.

The formula, "in the world but not of the world", in which Christians have usually been imprisoned and which is often used as a definition of the Christian, is now seen to be inadequate; it covers but a part of reality as if the term "Christian" signified

[20] H. de Lubac, *The Drama of Atheist Humanism* (London, 1945).
[21] P. Sidon, *L'esprit et l'histoire* (Paris, 1954), p. 112.

the supernatural relation without taking account of the *total* man who is involved in this relation. The relation of man with the world, as contained in the anthropology of the bible, appears more clearly than ever as a truly constitutive element in modern thought: "The world is not merely a universe of objects with which man starts a relationship as if he came from outside; it is much more; it is the condition that makes it possible for a human being to be himself." [22] To be in the world, therefore, does not mean to face the world or to be surrounded by it but rather to be with it in a mutually constitutive relationship. On the other hand, the world as a datum, taken up by man and transformed by him throughout history, has a solidity of its own, an intrinsic meaning that makes it intelligible through a whole list of projects with purposes that have a value of their own: science, art, communal organization, etc.

Immersed by his state of life in the very stuff of creation, the layman is most intimately linked up with it and has a direct hold of its meaning. Through marriage, scientific research, political and social activity and economic undertakings, *he participates in the very mystery of human nature and the world*. And so he confronts the Church, of which he is as much a citizen as of the world,[23] with the question as to the meaning of these secular activities and values for the history of salvation, i.e., the question of the relation between creation and redemption.

Moreover, it is not enough for him merely to ask a question, he also contributes part of the answer. For he shows, indeed, that ecclesiology and dogmatic theology as a whole cannot do without a theology of the realities of this earth because of the nature of things and the unity of reality. The emergence of the secular world as such, its unfolding according to its own internal laws, its claim to autonomy over against a Christendom that denied and refused it, the proof it has given of the legitimacy of this claim by the undeniable value of so many achievements and

[22] J.-Y. Jolif, "Le monde. Remarque sur la signification du terme," in *Lum. et vie* 14 (1965), n. 73, pp. 43-44.
[23] The Council stated this twice in the *Pastoral Constitution on the Church in the Modern World*, nn. 40, 43.

ambitions, the purifying process it has imposed willy-nilly on religion and the Church—all this has forced theologians to become more fully aware of the object of redemption, to have a clearer idea of the concrete vastness of its scope and to take more serious account of texts that had been left on the fringe of their investigations. The result is that God's plan stands out more clearly. In the light of the creative dynamism of man's history, certain texts of the bible can now be understood in their full implication, an implication which they possessed but which the circumstances I have described had more or less sterilized. Thus, for example, the first chapter of Genesis, where the world is the universe created for man, transformed and humanized by him in view of a loving communion with God. And again, the first chapter of the gospel of St. John, where John tells us that the Word that has become flesh is the same Word through whom all things were made, and without whom not anything was made that was made (1, 3) and through whom the world has been made (1, 10). And those verses of St. Paul's epistle to the Colossians where he declares that all things have been created in him, by him and for him, whether visible or invisible, and that God wants to reconcile all things through him with himself, both those on earth and those in the heavens (1, 15-20). The Word incarnate who is the Word of redemption continues the work of the Word of creation: the personal identity does not allow us to separate the two kinds of activity.

In short, the secular achievements of man are forcing theologians to think again about creation and leading them to a fuller understanding of the christocentrism of the bible.[24] This brings with it a new look at their eschatology, required by a new awareness of the unity of the achievement created by man and the world, as proclaimed by St. Paul (Rom. 8, 19-21), and of the implications, for the universe, of Christ's resurrection and the resurrection of the body.[25]

[24] Cf. A. Grillmeier, "L'image du Christ dans la théologie d'aujourd'hui," in *Questions théologiques aujourd'hui* II (Paris, 1965), pp. 97-99 (*Fragen der Theologie heute,* ed. J. Feiner, J. Trütsch and F. Böckle, Zurich/Cologne, 1957).

[25] H. Urs von Balthasar, "Eschatologie," in *Questions théologiques* .   .

Ecclesiology must expand proportionately. In order to locate the layman in the life of the Church, it is necessary to find a better definition of the relations between the Church and the world, until now rather vague and too juridical, and particularly a better definition of the Church's mission. One can no longer do this as if the history of salvation were but a history of souls to be rescued from the wreck of creation: what is saved is this creation itself.

The mission of the Church as an institution therefore refers at the same time to Jesus Christ as its beginning and its end, and to the world whose distinctive nature, structures and meaning it must respect; and this distinctive nature of the world is precisely that it is God's creation. This mission has the character of a dialogue,[26] and this means that by its very nature it implies a two-way circuit, an exchange of *truths,* with the world. These truths may belong to different levels, the levels of nature and grace, but both are essential to our knowledge, our life and our witness. The whole People of God, clergy and laity, is responsible for this mission, and particularly for the image it presents of Christ and of creation, which is the object of Christ's salvation. This fact provides the theology of the realities of this earth with a foundation and justification.

At the same time this brings out the theological function of the *laity,* who are by their nature the interpreters of this creation; by his immediate participation in the mystery of this creation, the layman is an "unveiler", a "revealer", of the truth of nature throughout the ages. Thus being the point of juncture in the relationship between the Church and the world by the very exercise of his humanity, the layman fulfills a function that is essential to the Church's mission. The theology of earthly realities and dialogue are closely connected and the laity have an important part to play in it, because this kind of theology depends more than any other on the sciences and philosophy. It was not the purpose of the bible to teach mankind about the concrete nature of the things of this world, and the little it says about this

---

II, pp. 288ff., particularly pp. 292-95; A. Grillmeier, *art. cit.,* pp. 97-104.
   [26] Cf. Y. Congar, *art. cit.,* pp. 356-57.

is not always free from historical limitations.[27] It is up to man himself to explore his natural environment, to examine his own activity so that he can understand himself better, and to integrate his knowledge with what he knows from other sources about the purposes revealed by God. This undertaking requires a "new kind of theologian". The "specialist" of this kind of theology must be "a kind of scholar of cultural synthesis. He must be interested in almost everything; he must find his inspiration and support in an omnivorous appetite for facts simply because they are facts, and in an insatiable interest in all kinds of beings simply because they happen to exist. This characteristic is no doubt generally considered a modern feature, but for him it is on the contrary a distinctive and uniquely Christian feature, the obvious practical corollary to the basic biblical affirmation that this world is God's world. In short, he should aim at, and up to a point succeed in, becoming a kind of humanist who is intoxicated with God, a man to whom nothing in nature and nothing in man is alien because there is nothing in nature or man that does not belong to God. Only such a universal and profoundly Christian love of life can give us a genuinely 'catholic' theology of which our world and our culture are so sorely in need. The theme of theology is life, and this life must be lived to the full as an inexhaustible source of joy before it can be interpreted theologically".[28] This is by definition the task of the layman. Christian thought, which for so long has remained a one-sidedly clerical thought, must henceforward be elaborated by clergy and laity *together*.

Within the Church the layman is not merely at the receiving end; he also contributes and radiates because it is he who deciphers creation and it is he who turns the history of this creation into a history of salvation without alienation. It is from his central function in the divine dispensation that his whole spirituality should derive.

[27] C. Duquoc, *Eschatologie et réalités terrestres*, pp. 12-15.
[28] J. V. Langmead Casserley, *Absence du Christianisme* (tr. H. Rambaud, Desclée de Brouwer, 1957), pp. 123-44.

José-María González-Ruiz/*Barcelona, Spain*

A Spirituality for a Time of Uncertainty

The free circulation and expansion of a dynamic and historicist spirituality, such as the deepest vision of the bible postulates, has up to now been prevented by the enormous weight of the old Hellenic tradition.

The great "metaphysics" of the West—those of Plato, Aristotle, Augustine and Malebranche, for example—display coordinated constants of this spirituality of "preestablished transcendence". According to them, morality does not have to be developed; it exists prior to the thinker's reflection, and all he has to do is discover it. It is the sum total of laws derived in logical progression from the characteristics of the universe and the place man occupies in it.

The concept of preestablished morality has come under attack today from Marxist and existentialist humanism. "Man makes himself," says Sartre;[1] "he is not something already made; he makes himself by choosing his morality, and pressure of circumstances is such that he has no choice but to choose one."

The Czechoslovakian Marxist philosopher Karel Kosík asks likewise: "What does man work out in history? The design of providence? The march of necessity? The progress of liberty? In history man works himself out. The meaning of history is to

---

[1] *L'existentialisme est un humanisme* (Paris, 1965), p. 78.

be found in history itself; in history man explains himself to himself, and this historical explanation—the equivalent of the creation of man and of humanity—is the only meaning of history." [2] Kosík himself attributes this revolutionary anti-theological concept of history to none other than Cardinal Nicholas of Cusa who wrote, *"Non ergo activae creationis humanitatis alius extat finis quam humanitas"*—the active creation of humanity has no other end than humanity.

We must frankly acknowledge that, in the moral tradition that sociologically passes for Christian, the aspect of the "ready-made model", seen as the only possible basis for a valid moral order, has been overemphasized. This concept reduces the moral life of man to the mere carrying out of transcendent concrete laws, valid *a priori* and unchangeable in time and space. Basically, this anthropological vision implies a negation of history. Men would have no more bonds between them than a series of lines converging on one preestablished point; the human adventure would have no meaning. In the place of history it puts a gigantic bureaucratic system of the order of some preexisting absolute value, which can be God or Progress or Reason or any other illusion of the human mind written with a capital letter.

Those who refuse to accept this purely executive sense of man's creative activity do not claim that individual action is an absolute initiative in history, disconnected from the sum total of previous achievements or outside human confines. "If the first basic premise of history," Kosík continues, "is the fact that it is *made by man,* the second and equally basic premise is the need for *continuity* to exist in this making. History is possible only insofar as man is not always beginning anew and for the first time, but is continually linking himself to the work and results achieved by preceding generations." [3]

There is no space here for a detailed analysis of the failures—and achievements—of this "morality of the preestablished order"

---

[2] *Dialektika konkrétního;* It. tr.: *Dialettica del concreto* (Milan, 1965), p. 260.
[3] *Ibid.*, p. 261.

over the course of nearly 2,000 years of Christian tradition. I simply propose to go back to the fountainhead, to start from the historical sense of the spirituality of the bible itself. The religion of the bible differs radically from all other historical religions through its particular concept of "spirituality". While in other religions "spirituality"—man's relationship with God—is obtained at the price of a greater or lesser renunciation of the task of building up the human world, in the bible man is bound to God—"the image and likeness of God"—by virtue of his responsibility for the transformation of the cosmos in which he lives and has his being (Gen. 1, 26).

Now this task of "creating history" is imposed on man with all the consequences entailed by his creative autonomy. In fact, for the Semites, to "name" something was the equivalent of having the power to transform that thing. So in the story of the six days of creation God "names" what we could term the previous objective conditions of history: light, darkness, the firmament, the dry land, the waters, the sun, the moon. But the animals—the first object of man's intervention—he leaves unnamed. The God of the bible adopts a paradoxical attitude of expectancy toward man's transforming activity, ". . . to see what he would call them" (Gen. 2, 19).

In the context of world religions, as H. Duméry has clearly pointed out,[4] a further absolute novelty in the bible is that it presents history as revealing God; to whatever extent man is made responsible for the making of his own history, a God who presents man with a ready-made model for him to copy purely and simply is inconceivable within the framework of the biblical viewpoint. Neglect of man's creative responsibility in forming himself has tinged Christian spirituality with security and stability, very far from the true nomadic character of the great believers and prophets described in the bible.

[4] *Phénoménologie et religion* (Paris: P.U.F., 1962), p. 9.

I

Christian Spirituality Is a Bond
with a Transcendent and Gratuitous God

To speak of a transcendent God with whom man forms spiritual links is to oppose transcendence to immanence, but not to "incarnation". The strict monotheism of the bible continually emphasizes the transcendence of God, conceived as a radical resistance to the intra-creatural reducibility of divinity. God always has to remain outside the intrinsic web of human and worldly dynamism. There is no reason to consider God as an immanent explanation of the enigmas of the human mind or an intrinsic cog in the mesh of reality created in evolution.

Throughout the whole bible there appears, time after time, the anguished cry of the just man who meets with failure, constantly asking God why he has departed from him and left him at the mercy of the internal rhythm of history. Not even the greatest of the just who fail is exempt from this cry of interrogation. Jesus himself died repeating in anguish the lament of the psalmists and the prophets: "My God, my God, why hast thou forsaken me?"

The temptation to immanentize God so as to manipulate him to the tune of an ordered sequence of events is described in the bible as belonging to the very infra-structure of human history: in the middle of the Garden of Eden stands the tree of universal knowledge ("of good and evil"), and the tempter assures man that just by stretching out his hand and eating the fruit of the tree he will immediately obtain what would otherwise be the end result of a long and difficult process of elaboration (Gen. 2, 17; 3, 2-4). Man commits the sin of "magic"; he uses a device to hasten the process and abuses religion so as to free himself from the charge laid upon him of building up history with the resources given him.

Religion becomes a force of "alienation" to the degree that the believer abandons the uncomfortable position of being bound to the absolutely transcendent. Men try to scale God down so as to fit him into a pattern of immediate utility and offer him the place of honor on the boards of all great human enterprises.

Now this being bound to the absolutely transcendent has to be achieved in a dialectical rhythm, a difficult rhythm to which human laziness often refuses to adjust. The biblical God, the "utterly other", is not absent from the dynamics of human history; on the contrary, he constantly impinges on it and involves himself in the affairs of men without ever coming to belong to them. The transcendent God of the bible is the God of Abraham, Isaac and Jacob. "Yet he is not far from each one of us, for 'in him we live and move and have our being'" (Acts 17, 27-28; cf. Is. 55, 6; Ps. 145, 18; Rom. 1, 19).

But his presence is completely gratuitous. There is nothing in the intrinsic mechanism of the cosmos or the course of history that needs God as the immanent explanation of being or becoming. In the bible we constantly find God described as the one who is coming—God is *ho erchómenos*—knocking at the door of human consciousness when least expected, coming like a thief in the night (Mt. 24, 43; Lk. 12, 39; 1 Thess. 5, 2; 2 Pet. 3, 10; Apoc. 3, 3; 16, 15). The biblical God is a "thief-God" whose presence cannot be taken into account in the daily run of domestic economy.

This dialectical tension between transcendence and incarnation can be broken by an undue emphasis on one aspect or another. In the first place, there is a sort of sin of excessive emphasis on transcendence: God, being utterly other, requires of those who adore him a complete or at least partial estrangement from their spatio-temporal context. Religion then retreats into "places of worship"; these form federations and become hallowed precincts within whose walls a life of evasion and flight is carried on. The religious man becomes someone literally "set apart", someone who organizes the administration of his life within the confines of a *sacra civitas*.

In the history of Christian spirituality this pole of evasion and estrangement can easily be recognized in religious orders and various schools of perfection. They give the impression that man lives in an autonomous religious universe, somewhere beyond which dwells the profane sphere, and a heavy entrance fee is normally demanded at the frontiers of the religious universe.

An inevitable consequence of this excess is an over-valuation of grace. The possession of grace becomes a key to human fulfillment, which in some way dispenses its owner from the need to use other instruments of progress and advancement. The option for "the one thing necessary" is constantly preached. It is this that Marxist humanism is criticizing in its stricture on religion as "the opium of the people".

This "transcendentalist" excess of Christian spirituality has its hidden psychological motivation in a desperate search for security. The Polish Marxist philosopher Hans Schaff has made a subtle analysis of this *embourgoisement* of religion: "For a believer the question is very simple: life always has a meaning— i.e., it is worth living, under any conditions—since even suffering, pain and death are in conformity with the designs of the superior being who will compensate for the sufferings of this life in the afterlife or who has decided to inflict these terrestrial punishments for sins committed. Let us admit that in many circumstances—and in this case too—it is very comfortable to be a believer; the most difficult questions become excessively simple. But the price paid for this comfort is a crushing one: the renunciation of all scientific enquiry. Precisely for this reason it seems continually more difficult to allow oneself the luxury of such 'comforts' and simplifications." [5]

In its attempts to avoid this transcendentalist excess, Christian spirituality shows, over its nearly 2000 years of history, numerous examples of the opposite extreme: an excess of "incarnationalism". The hermit emerges brusquely from his cell and at one fell swoop sets himself to control the destinies of the secular *civitas*. An attempt at "reconciliation" with the "world" is made, but this is accompanied by an attitude of more or less barefaced paternalism toward it.

[5] *Filosofia czlowieka;* Sp. tr.: *La filosofía del hombre* (Buenos Aires, 1964), p. 74.

This process of "incarnational extremism" got off to a flying start with the Peace of Constantine and reached its apogee in the grandiose structure of medieval Christendom. When secular values started their struggle to free themselves from the yoke of religion in the 14th century, a long process of secularization was begun, which has still not fully worked itself out. The remains of this subjugation of the secular field to the religious can be seen in the sectarian attitudes that still affect important areas of economic, social and political life.

The *Pastoral Constitution on the Church in the Modern World* is a difficult and painful attempt to rid Christian spirituality of this unreasonable pretension; however, we must remember that "the world" will need abundant evidence of a change of heart before it is convinced that this is not just a piece of tactical opportunism designed to enable the Church to overcome the crisis of secularization. This "opening-up" of the Church is still regarded as a flirtation with the adversary aimed at obtaining a truce. This is how the Soviet philosopher F. V. Konstantinov sees it: "In our day, religion and the Church are still the implacable enemies of science, which does not prevent the Vatican and other religious institutions from flirting with it and trying to 'reconcile' scientific discoveries with religious dogmas. . . . The Catholic Church is a powerful political organization, with endless ramifications and a wealth of capital, property and other assets. Its center, the Vatican, is a corporation looking for spiritual take-over bids and the social exploitation of many nations. It supported the Fascist regimes and today is the ally of every sort of reaction. It supports reactionary plots. The Vatican uses Christian or Catholic political parties and other Catholic organizations to put its reactionary policies into force. In order to strengthen its influence over the workers and intensify its fight against communism, the Church puts forth the false notion of so-called 'Christian socialism', makes extensive use of demagogy and in fact acts as a spiritual stranglehold in the hands of the exploiting classes." [6]

[6] *Fundamentos de la filosofía marxista* (Mexico,[2]1965), pp. 585ff.

Whatever elements of truth this view may contain, it must be recognized that in Vatican Council II the Catholic Church has clearly defined the principles of its "temporal incarnation" and roundly condemned those incarnational excesses that largely justify criticisms such as the above.

Above all, it roundly condemns "clerical domination" of the political actions of Catholics: laymen must "realize that their pastors will not always be so expert as to have a ready answer to every problem (even every grave problem) that arises; this is not the role of the clergy. . . . They ought to remember that in those cases no one is permitted to identify the authority of the Church exclusively with his own opinion".[7] At the same time, the Church states that it is not its role to produce technical solutions to problems of social structure, but to limit itself humbly and religiously to witnessing "the birth of a new humanism, where man is defined first of all by his responsibility toward his brothers and at the court of history".[8]

As Catholics we cannot but lament the gulf that still yawns between these forthright official declarations of the Church and the actions of so many of our most representative institutions. The word "Catholic", or even "Christian", is still strongly associated with numerous institutional forms of reaction in economic, social, cultural and political fields. Most lamentable of all is that the spirit of clerical domination, which still survives among us, imposes and propagates a spirituality based on bourgeois and neo-capitalist securities, and even offers them a transcendental justification.

Both tendencies—toward transcendentalist or incarnationalist excesses—are frequently united in a hidden infra-structure on which they ultimately rest. As so often happens, extremes meet. And the common element that brings them together is, without doubt, the desperate search for spiritual security. Man has a tendency to set himself once and for all in a fixed and secure position, and to rebel against the only possible stance

[7] *Pastoral Constitution on the Church in the Modern World*, n. 43.
[8] *Ibid.*, n. 55.

which the true believer must maintain every day and almost every minute: that of dialectical tension between transcendence and incarnation.

The more religious a man is, the more human will his basic attitude to life be; but he will never use his religion as an instrument of dominion or monopoly in the marketplace of different social, economic or political techniques.

II

CHRISTIAN "RELIGIOSITY" IS PRIMARILY ANTHROPO-CENTRAL

A common error of perspective in the world of Christian spirituality is to place the foreground of the believer's ethical and mystical impulses in God, and only through God in the world and in man.

This has led atheistic humanism, both Marxist and existentialist, to reproach Christianity with nothing less than destroying love of one's neighbor. In effect, if I love my neighbor simply and exclusively because he is an incarnation and representation of God it is not man that I am loving, but God in man. Man fades away before the image of God; he becomes no more than a peg on which to hang the only interesting reality, God. My neighbor will feel humiliated and degraded, sensing that he as a person is of no interest to me, except as a sort of "recommendation" from a superior being.

This misdirection of focus in love of one's neighbor can be seen in the practice of many religious institutions that are dedicated by their statutes precisely to love of neighbor. The "neighbor", the object of the cares and solicitudes of "professional do-gooders", is shown, explicitly or implicitly, that his concrete human reality counts for nothing: all that counts is his transparency that allows the divinity to shine through the fragility of his existence.

This can easily lead to a real lack of interest in the tragedy of man, the professed object of the charity. He is frequently made to feel that if it were not for the fact that he represents God, he would not deserve any attention whatsoever. This explains the "angelism" of many so-called Christian attitudes toward human reality. We boast about not knowing the tragedies of our neighbors, because in fact all that concerns us is this misunderstood presence of God in our neighbor.

And yet, throughout the whole of the bible, the opposite view is constantly in evidence. God himself interests himself in man precisely on account of his reality as man. There is a prophetic current running through the bible which continually reproaches men for trying to find a direct short cut to God without passing through love of neighbor.

It is easy for the believer to succumb to the temptation to establish a direct link with the divinity without treading the high road of contact with his neighbor. And so, a spirituality of pure transcendence grows up, taking refuge in the temple as a place of complete security. This is the spirituality of "liturgical security" which the prophet Jeremiah described in such vigorous terms (Jer. 7, 1-7). Jeremiah roundly states that *before* going into the temple, you must proceed along the only possible route of effective attention to your neighbor. This involves a recognition that God is found through one's neighbor, and not one's neighbor through God. The neighbor is considered as something with a prior existence of his own and worthy of being valued for himself.

It is interesting to note that this "theocentrism condemned by the prophet is clearly tied to a spirituality of certitude and security: "Will you steal, murder, commit adultery, swear falsely, burn incense to Baal, and go after other gods that you have not known, and then come and stand before me in this house, which is called by my name, and say: 'We are delivered!' —only to go on doing all these abominations?" (Jer. 7, 9-10).

The neighbor is considered so autonomous in biblical spirituality that the route passing through him is held to be sufficient for eschatological salvation itself, even when it does not explicitly lead to the high road to God. In Matthew 25, 31-46, the Son of Man will recognize as his all those who serve their neighbors, even when they have not expressly recognized him in them. This is the only way to explain the question that the "good" will ask in surprise: "Lord, when was it that we saw thee hungry, and fed thee, or thirsty, and gave thee drink?" (Mt. 25, 37).

Having rid ourselves of this gross error, we must not allow ourselves to forget that our "neighbor", as an object of Christian love, is precisely a representation of God, an authentic incarnation of God. This is why the "neighbor" participates in the gratuitousness and transcendence of God, dialectically combined with his incarnation.

Our neighbor in the Christian sense is, in the first place, somehow gratuitous and transcendent. Love of our neighbor does not compete with the corresponding techniques of hominization which jostle each other in the marketplace of the different forms of humanism. It would be a mistake to imagine love of one's neighbor as a sort of universal panacea, dispensing man from his task of individual and collective auto-creation. Christian love goes beyond all human presuppositions without thereby invalidating them.

The concept of neighbor transcends the bonds of flesh, geography, race, culture and politics. The neighbor bursts into everyone's life, outside the bounds of all provisions and beyond the scope of all planning. The great novelty of the Christian message is the duty to "prove oneself a neighbor" to others—the parable of the Good Samaritan. Neighbors cannot be chosen, but they are accepted at even the most inopportune moments.

The transcendence and gratuitousness of the neighbor should show itself in a sort of allergy to institutionalization. In the same way that throughout the history of Christian spirituality men have tried to immanentize God, belittling him and trying to fit him into the framework of human comprehension, so they have tried to reduce love of one's neighbor to a set of minutely detailed rules that remove the element of surprise and insecurity from life.

This produces the not infrequent case of religious institutions, created to mold this love of neighbor into shape, which have come to the point when they plan every act of love in such detail that they leave no room for the real neighbor, who by definition transcends all calculations and provisions.

At a time like the present, when fortunately many of the causes of human insecurity are disappearing, "love of one's neighbor" is even more useful than ever. The tangled web of coordinated securities—which wrap man up to such an extent that spontaneous action becomes impossible—can only be broken in the name of absolute fortuitousness and transcendence.

However, love of one's neighbor, though resistant to immanentism, is not something abstract and distant either, but must, on the contrary, become incarnate by acting on concrete and immediate reality. We Christians have to love human beings in their unpredictable and concrete reality.

The first thing this "incarnate" love requires is to be completely in tune with men of our time and with our surroundings. An "angelist" spirituality—by making man lose his sense of history, sending him chasing, like Don Quixote, after ways of life and ages long dead and gone—seriously fails in this task of making Christian love incarnate.

This means that many of our monastic, religious and even lay institutions that seek a sort of "spiritual" security through abstracting themselves from contemporary events, will have to be revised. The absolute ban on the reading of newspapers in some religious houses, for example, can easily prevent the members from carrying out their inescapable duty of being in tune with the times, which is absolutely necessary for genuine love of one's neighbor.

Here we have to face the very real question of "compromising with the times" which is such a burning problem today for the best of active Christians. At one moment full of fight for the advancement of humanity, the next moment they find themselves drawing back for fear of "compromising" their essentially Christian identity by involvement in the immediate present, and in doing so appear to others as an equivocal and evasive witness in the search for new and more just historical orientations. In fact, love of one's neighbor as a typically Christian product requires for its realization a sort of dialectical tension between transcendence and incarnation.

The parable of the Good Samaritan (Lk. 10, 25-37) gives an excellent outline for the understanding of this dialectical equilibrium. On the one hand, the "neighbor" was something unforeseen and unforeseeable; the priest and the Levite passed him by because they could not see in their liturgical agenda any place for this unforeseen demand for help. They thereby renounced the transcendence of love of one's neighbor. At the same time, the samaritan did not try to comply with the normal demands of the Welfare State by the money he gave the innkeeper; he was not organizing a fund for those found wounded by the wayside; on the contrary, he understood that to "show himself a neighbor" he had to come close to a particular individual in a particular situation.

III

CONCLUSION

This brief survey has shown that Christian spirituality is essentially a spirituality of insecurity, even in times of certainty, which ours most certainly is not. In a time of uncertainty like ours this inevitable dialectical tension between transcendence and incarnation, which characterizes genuine Christian spirituality, needs to be stressed.

In the *Pastoral Constitution on the Church in the Modern World,* the need for this continuous process of setting up and taking down the very fabric of our religious universe is explicitly recognized: "The accelerated pace of history is such that one can scarcely keep abreast of it. Hitherto the destiny of mankind as a whole consisted of the fragmentary annals of various peoples: now it merges into a complete whole. And so mankind substitutes a dynamic and more evolutionary concept of nature for a static one and the result is an immense series of new problems calling for a new endeavor of analysis and synthesis." [9]

The new efforts of analysis and synthesis required are bound to entail a painful effort. Perhaps the resistance we put up to setting out on this dialectical road is due in large part to the undoubted entrenchment of the Church in bourgeois forms and modes of life.

I think this is the moment to shake the consciences of Christians out of this, the moment for them to set out on the true road that all real believers have trod in the wake of the father of them all, Abraham, who, when God called him to seek the land he was to receive as his inheritance, set out *without knowing where he was going*.

[9] *Ibid.*, n. 5.

Pierre Reginald Cren, O.P./*Eveux, France*

The Christian and the World according to Teilhard de Chardin

Having examined the "signs of the times", and recognized that "the human race is today living through a new age in its history", the Church has described this new atmosphere as the transition from "a predominantly static notion of the order of things to a more dynamic and evolutionary conception", giving rise to "a new situation". Now that it is at last "really and intimately involved" in the human adventure,[1] the Church in council has declared that its pastoral role must be one of dialogue with the world. And all this has taken place exactly ten years after the death of a man whose life and thought were an untiring witness to the importance of this dialogue. Today this witness still remains as a guide to the new, yet traditional, spiritual attitude which the Christian, who is faithful to both earth and heaven, must now possess. As time moves on, leaving in its wake the discarded fruits of unrestrained enthusiasm and self-interested controversy, the atmosphere has become more relaxed and we have been given time for thought. Now that the publication of Teilhard de Chardin's letters and early writings has enabled us to share in his initial and most personal experiences, and his whole achievement at last analyzed philosophically and theologically

[1] Cf. introduction and preliminary exposition of the *Constitution on the Church* (Glen Rock, N.J.: Paulist Press, 1964).

73

in truly great commentaries,[2] it becomes possible to say with confidence, without being immediately suspected of blindness to his shortcomings, that Teilhard de Chardin is a true master of present-day spirituality.

The Problem

The problem of the compatibility or radical opposition between the love of God and the love of the world is not exempt from a certain imbalance. In reading some theological or spiritual writers, it very soon becomes apparent that the side of the equation representing the world is not really present because it has never really been lived. Under the weighty influence of the monastic spirituality of flight from the world, whose prophetic value Teilhard never denied, but whose claims to exclusiveness must be challenged, the world is *a priori* a source of temptation and then an object of repulsion. And often through lack of involvement in human responsibilities, the priest, the director of conscience, has only a merely theoretical understanding of what the world is. On the other hand, the disastrous divorce between spirituality and theology stands in the way of the genuine integration of mysticism and profane action into an all-embracing synthesis, which alone can help us to appreciate fully the relationship existing between them.

In contrast, Teilhard de Chardin's "ascetical and mystical teaching" is characterized by a real and almost innate involvement in the world of the laboring earth and the world of God. The problem of their reconciliation is not something standing outside himself. For him it is so essential that the history of his life and thought merge into the history of its first intimations

---

[2] Cf. M. Barthélémy-Madaule, *Bergson et Teilhard de Chardin* (Paris, 1963); H. de Lubac, *La pensée religieuse du Père Teilhard de Chardin* (Paris, 1963); idem. *La prière du Père Teilhard de Chardin* (Paris, 1964); tr.: *Teilhard de Chardin: The Man and His Meaning* (New York, 1965); P. Smulders, *La vision de Teilhard de Chardin* (Paris, 1964); E. Rideau, *La pensée du Père Teilhard de Chardin* (Paris, 1965). All these works treat of our theme at length. It would have been necessary to make constant reference to the excellent analyses they contain, but we shall just refer to them this once so as not to multiply the notes.

and its solution over the years.[3] He revealed this many times. "The originality of my belief is that it has its roots in two spheres of life which are usually looked upon as being mutually antagonistic. By education and intellectual formation, I belong to 'the children of heaven'. But by temperament and professional studies, I am 'a child of the earth'. Placed thus by life at the heart of two worlds, whose outlook, language and opinions I know through intimate experience, I have set up no inner dividing wall. But I have let two apparently contradictory influences react in perfect freedom, one upon the other, in the depths of my being. Now at the end of this process, after thirty years devoted to the pursuit of inner unity, I have the impression that a synthesis has taken place, in a natural way, between the two streams that make their demands upon me." [4]

The pursuit of inner unity, without doubt, constitutes the central core of Teilhard's development throughout his whole life. "There can be no question about one point, namely, my anxious concern to unify my inner life, which I feel too acutely for many others not to have experienced just like me." [5] Here, in one sentence, Teilhard gives expression to his abiding conviction that the conflict between the love of God and the love of the earth, where he acted as God's "testing ground",[6] far from being a problem peculiar to his own spiritual life, in fact constitutes the central debate. This brings the human race, conscious of its tasks and blinded by a Promethean religion, into conflict with the Church, the bearer of ultimate light, but,

[3] It is "the problem of my life" (*Mon. Univers.* [1918] = *Ecrits du temps de la guerre* [Paris, 1965], p. 278).

[4] *Comment Je crois* (1934): P. Teilhard de Chardin, *Je m'explique* (Paris, 1966), p. 213. "The two components [the love of God and faith in the world] are everywhere 'in the air', but usually not sufficiently powerful, both of them at the same time, to combine one with the other in the same subject. In me, by pure chance (temperament, education, background), the proportion of one to the other being found favorable, the fusion took place spontaneously. . . ." (*Le Christique* [1955]: *Je m'explique*, p. 220).

[5] *Mon Univers* (1918) = *Ecrits*, p. 278.

[6] *Lettres à Leontine Zanta* (Paris, 1965), p. 76: "It would already have been much to have served God as a testing ground for this wonderful marriage of the loves of heaven and the earth" (August 28, 1926).

since the Renaissance, cut off from the living forces that give birth to a new world.[7] The problem of interior unification is what is at stake in the Christian apostolate.

The evolution of this inner unification, which was not to be achieved without a struggle, started from a fundamental experience of extraordinary intensity, whose implications Teilhard, throughout his life, was to develop, clarify and systematize in his theoretical writings. Here he tried to convey the full meaning of his initial and abiding vision, but without ever being perfectly successful. But in the wartime writings, *Les Ecrits du temps de la guerre*, that time of "blossoming of ideas, of intellectual honeymoon",[8] his essential experience is disclosed to us with an ardent lyricism which, far from being a merely superficial ornament, shows how deeply he had been stirred in the deepest recesses of his soul. In *La Vie Cosmique* (1916), Teilhard's "first paper of some consequence", where "we assist at a kind of spiritual crystallization, at the birth of a synthesis which is sketched out quite completely and all at once",[9] the problem is posed: "For no one so much as the Christian, that is, for him who kneels before a cross and to whom an adored voice repeats: 'Leave all to possess all', is the choice presented so burdened with hesitation and anguish.[10] Ultimately, to be a Christian, must we renounce being human, human in the fullest and deepest sense of the word, greedily and passionately human? To follow Jesus, must we renounce the hope that we touch and dispose of a little of the Absolute every time that, as a result of our labors, a little more determinism is mastered, a little more truth acquired and a little more progress realized?" [11]

---

[7] Cf., for example, *La Maîtrise du monde et le Règne de Dieu = Ecrits*, pp. 67ff.

[8] *Lettres à L. Zanta*, p. 57.

[9] C. D'Armagnac, "Le premier Teilhard," in *Etudes* (1966), p. 654; *Revue Teilhard de Chardin* (Perspectives), n. 23, p. 23.

[10] We know that the problem presented itself to Teilhard de Chardin in an acute form during his religious novitiate and was resolved thanks to the "solid common sense" of his novice-master. Cf. C. Cuénot, *P. Teilhard de Chardin, les grandes étapes de son évolution* (Paris, 1958), p. 19.

[11] *Ecrits*, pp. 7-8.

The Solution: The Initial Experience of Synthesis

The dilemma was to be overcome so that God and the world would be reconciled together, not by some pious artifice, but as a result of a religious experience into which a scientific attitude, metaphysical perception and a theological approach to reality all flowed and were blended together, reaching new depths in the process. Among the war texts, in which he tried to describe this original intuition of synthesis,[12] one of the most characteristic is *The Divine Milieu* (1917). Here we have a description of the five concentric circles which determine the atmosphere in which the soul, stirred by the cosmic sense, is bathed:[13] a soul already conscious, "as of a presence", "of a radical, ontological and total drift of the universe" all around it,[14] and searching passionately for the Absolute and the ultimate reality.[15]

The first circle is the circle of Presence.[16] Beyond the glitter of appearances the omnipresence of God is recognized. "What you saw passing by like a world, behind a song, behind a tinge of color, behind the eyes, is not here or there; it is a Presence spread around everywhere. . . . We are still able to say nothing about this diffused Reality, except that it is and that it envelops, and that mysteriously it beautifies." But this Reality, which is revealed through sensation, is none other than God, the "divine immanent", who is also uncompromisingly "the Other". Out of this experience two consequences follow. Since the cosmos is a transparency of the divine, the place and medium

[12] M. Barthélémy-Madaule has analyzed, as a philosopher, the significance of this initial intuition of synthesis. Cf. *op. cit.*, pp. 19ff., 79ff., etc.

[13] Cf. *Je m'explique*, pp. 161-62. The cosmic sense is a religious sense. For Teilhard de Chardin the approach to nature is religious. "If I have always loved and scrutinized nature, I can now say that it was not as a scholar, but as a 'dévot'. It seems to me that, in my case, every effort, even bearing on a purely natural object, has always been a religious and essentially unique effort" (*Mon Univers [1918] = Ecrits*, p. 270).

[14] *Le Coeur de la Matière* (1950), Part I, p. 3.

[15] *Mon Univers (1918) = Ecrits*, p. 269.

[16] Unless otherwise indicated, all the texts quoted in this second part are taken from *Le Milieu Mystique = Ecrits*, pp. 137-67; Eng. tr.: *The Divine Milieu* (New York: Harper & Row, 1960).

of this first revelation of God, and since sensation has been its intermediary channel, how is it that to encounter the Savior one must flee the world and repudiate its whole sensitive aspect? No, on the contrary, "if a man desires to raise up within himself, for God, the structure of a sublime love, he must above all develop his sensitive faculties. Through a prudent but assiduous interchange with the most stimulating realities, he must carefully nourish within himself the feelings, the vision and taste of the Omnipresence with which all things in nature are haloed". Moreover, through this discovery of the divine Immanence in all things and in himself, the world with its infinitely varied faces is suddenly brought into unity in God and at the same moment makes possible a first unification of the soul.[17]

The approach to God through the cosmos moves deeper in the second circle: the circle of Consistency. "Under the unifying action of the universal Presence, the soul sees that the Real has become not only transparent but *solid*. The incorruptible principle of the cosmos has now been discovered, and it is diffused everywhere." "In an instant, the workaday but imponderable surface sheen of things, through which the inner reality common to all things is lighted up, becomes now the universal Consistency in which all of us subsist and move." God is no longer just the one who allows himself to be contemplated; he is the one in whom, through the cosmos, we must abandon ourselves, for he is its Consistency. From now on the delusion of appearances and the pain of contingency, the flower that fades and the trials that come, are of little consequence: "You alone are solid, O my God." But the omnipresent and consistent God is also the one who acts.

In the third circle, the circle of Energy, the mystic has an experience of God the creator, whose act of creation is for us "a mighty, continuous gesture, spaced out over the totality of time", causing "the world, ceaselessly though imperceptibly, to

---

[17] Unification from the manifold: a fundamental theme of his thought and the central point around which revolves his reflections on creation and on the spiritual life. Cf., for example, *La lutte contre la Multitude* (1917) and *L'Union créatrice* (1917) = *Ecrits*, pp. 113-32, 175-97.

emerge just a shade above nothingness". "Over the whole surface and through the depths of the cosmos, it is God's action that shapes us like the clay of the first day. Then the mystic meditates in the sacred communion of the omni-operating Will." In all he endures—suffering, failure and death—it is the hand of God that is lovingly seized. But there is "a new way, more perfect than suffering, to cleave to the divine influence . . . communion in action". Through his inner purification, his submissiveness to human duty and to grace, through the development of his thought, the expansion of his heart, the intensification of his external activity, the mystic tends to be merged more and more with the creative action.[18]

Let us pause and look back for a moment on the path trodden so far through mystical experience. One might be tempted to say that there is nothing original in asserting that the cosmic sense is the starting point for encountering the omnipresent and omniagent God, and that the way explored by Teilhard de Chardin is analogous to that which has traditionally undergirded the elaboration of the great theologies of God as one and the creator, especially that of St. Thomas Aquinas. However, it does deserve to hold our attention at a time when, under the influence of disruptive philosophies and theologies, some of which, moreover, wish to acquiesce in the claims of scientific analysis, we have forgotten about the reference from the creature to the creator and, through fear of all forms of immanentism, obscured the sense of the immanent God, "in whom we live and move and have our being".

It is no doubt remarkable to record that it was a true man of science who rediscovered God in the cosmos and who has shown us again the natural roots of religious experience.[19] The

[18] These themes are developed in *The Divine Milieu, op. cit.*

[19] The reason for this is that the scientific approach of Teilhard de Chardin moves beyond pure analysis into an act of synthesis which perceives things in their totality. Cf. *Science et Christ ou Analyse et Synthèse = Oeuvres,* IX (Paris, 1965), pp. 45ff., where he establishes that: "1. The scientific study of the world, which is essentially analytical, makes us first of all move in the opposite direction to divine realities; 2. . . . it is precisely this scientific penetration into things, by revealing

first three circles of the *"divine milieu"* were always to remain for him the first resting places of his Interior Castle.[20] "Domine, fac ut Te videam, ut Te *omnipraesentem* et *omnianimantem* videam et sentiam" (1945). However, the vision is still not yet complete. Indeed, it is so one-sided that Teilhard goes so far as to describe it as "an awakened dream", "an undeveloped vision, disagreeably riddled with dualism, externalism and fixism".

What does it lack? The realization that the cosmos is not only the transparency of the divine Presence and the ground for its action, but that also it is itself the very Object that God gradually penetrates through, so as to divinize it. The emergence of this new understanding of the divine action, made possible by a consciousness of cosmic evolution, was a decisive fact in Teilhard's experience. The history of the cosmos, of transforming and recapitulating creation, is the history of a divinization. What is built up through the course of time is not God, but, a divine reality, his reign. The energy present from the beginning to concentrate multiplicity into unity through successive steps and which stirs up the desire of the sons of the earth for progress is really the energy of God leading back all things to himself, so as to make a divine milieu of the recapitulated cosmic whole by means of a completely gratuitous metamorphosis. In this conception God no longer reveals himself only as the On High, or as the Within of things, but also as the Beyond. At the end of creation's evolutionary Odyssey, it is still God who appears. So now the task of the man who wishes to unite himself to God no longer consists only in contemplating the Omnipresent under the surface of things, of allowing himself to be taken over by the Omniagent and acting in conformity with him —his task now is to take possession of the earth, so as to bring it successfully to the divine end that God has destined for it and

---

to us the synthetic structure of the world, which leads us to make an about-face and projects us through its natural extension toward the unique center of things which is God our Lord" (*ibid.,* pp. 47-48.

[20] This comparison with the Interior Castle of St. Theresa has often been made.

whose coming God has prepared for from the beginning of time with a faultless logic. "Now that human endeavor no longer just concerns him as an operation merging with the divine action, but as Work (*opus*) conditioning the presence of God among us; now that it becomes possible for him, not only to feel the divine milieu, but to fashion it and to surround himself with it, as with a light of ever-increasing density; now that, so as to adhere to God, it is no longer sufficient to give himself to action just to act, but he must give himself to action to succeed, he [the mystic], with no effort on his part, is imbued with the relentless ardor for progress which impassions the sons of the earth."

In the fourth circle, the reconciliation between the love of God and the love of the earth seems to have been brought about. The mystic has no more fears of being an escapist or a dreamer. He is rather the most realistic of men, for now in his quest for God he must embrace the whole of the Real.

Nevertheless, as long as the figure of Jesus has not appeared, nothing decisive has yet been said. In the fifth circle of the divine milieu this figure appears, recapitulating both the world and mystical experience. "I have seen a shadow passing by. . . . What is the name of this mysterious Entity which is a little our work and with which above all we commune; which is something of ourselves and which yet holds us in subjection; which has need of us to be and which at the same time dominates us with his whole Absolute? . . . I feel it. It has a name and a face. But it alone can reveal itself and give its name as . . . Jesus."

The parables of the *Coeur de la Matière* (1916)[21] show us how he resolved the problem of the universal character of Christ, that haunted him so much: "A Christ who reached only a part of the universe, a Christ who did not in some way sum up (or was not) the world, would seem to me a Christ who was smaller than the Real. . . . The God of our faith would ap-

[21] *Ecrits*, pp. 85ff.; *Hymne de l'Univers* (Paris, 1961), pp. 39ff.; Eng. tr.: *Hymn of the Universe* (New York: Harper & Row, 1965).

pear to me to be less great than the universe of our experience." [22] The face of the omnipresent and omniagent God who allows himself to be known in the beauty and the energies of the cosmos is the face of Christ. Consistency—it is he "in quo omnia constant". The God of the Beyond, the center of convergence and the focus of attraction of the whole of creation—it is he. And the divine reality which has been built up throughout the history of the cosmos with the assistance of human labor—again, it is he: "the synthesis of the created universe and its creator" [23]—this is the pleroma of him in whom everything must be recapitulated, "the mysterious reality that we can no longer describe as God alone (since God could pass from the world), but that we can no longer think of as absolutely gratuitous, absolutely unessential, without making creation incomprehensible, the passion of Christ something absurd and our effort devoid of interest".[24] Now the link of the mystical experience of the relations between God and the universe has been drawn tight.[25] No longer are there two juxtaposed and contradictory worlds in the soul. The encounter with God and the construction of the world no longer stand in contradiction. It is possible to unite the passion of the earth and the passion of God without inner strain and without inner division.

If we have paid particular attention to the description of this mystical itinerary, whose early imperfect expression was later to achieve greater clarity, but which was to underlie the life and achievement of Teilhard de Chardin, this is because we see it as his fundamental contribution to the spiritual history of our time. Whoever wishes to understand the full meaning of his witness should study not so much the theoretical works, no matter how

---

[22] *Mon Univers (1918)* = *Ecrits*, p. 273.
[23] *Ibid.*, p. 272.
[24] *Mon Univers (1924)*: *Oeuvres*, IX, p. 114.
[25] The mystical experience of the relationship between God and the universe does not constitute the whole of mysticism. For Teilhard de Chardin it is ultimately only an introduction to the mysticism of the personal dialogue of the soul with its God, of "the loving initiation of a person to another unfathomable presence". Cf. the conclusion of *The Divine Milieu*, op. cit., pp. 69-121.

imposing they might be and which are still an inadequate expression of his basic intuition, but rather the intimations of his mystical experience. Here we see that the problem of the compatibility of a complete human involvement and an unconditional faithfulness to God was solved without compromise, through an interior pilgrimage, bathed in prayer, which led Teilhard de Chardin to sanctity. No one who has read his spiritual notes can have any doubts about this. Through this experience he became a spiritual master of our day, and he invites us to follow the same path. Philosophical and theological discussions about particular aspects of his thought, however necessary and fruitful they might be, are always in danger of being irrelevant, so long as the evidence of his inner experience is not understood. What is essential is first of all and always to "see".

The Spiritual Vision: Moving toward a Theology

The spiritual vision touched on the truth, for at last it had grasped the coherency of the Real. Every true mystical experience is an intuitive synthesis of the whole. It is a perceiving, all in the same act, of God and the world and of the relationship between them. In one continuous movement, it moves beyond a rigidly dualistic conception of reality and apprehends the living unity of all things in God. And at the same time it realizes at a glance that from the beginning of time to the appearance of the new earth and the new heaven, one and the same adventure is being pursued. It never pauses to consider the individual stage for its own sake, although it never denies it. For only the completed whole is the bearer of revelation. Creation has no meaning outside of Christ who is incarnate within it and who brings it to consummation, and the significance of the cross escapes the person who does not see it taken up into the resurrection and the formation of the mystical and cosmic pleroma, right up until the final end when "God will be the All in all".

By reason of its movement gathering all into synthesis, the spiritual vision that reconciles the love of God and the love of the world is a movement toward a theology of the whole in which the living bond between God and his creation will be wholly and perfectly expressed. That is why, because of his inner experience, the fundamental purpose inspiring his whole endeavor is a truly theological desire for a truly comprehensive theology.[26] Not that he ever mixed up the different levels, in particular those of scientific investigation and theological reflection, by giving in to the temptation of concordism. But he brought out their continuity, through the necessity for coherence, that is, of truth and of theological truth. Those individualistic and sectarian theologies, in which present-day Christian reflection runs the risk of being entangled, are not capable of expressing and satisfying true spiritual experience or of throwing light on the problem of the place of the Christian in the world. Only some great theological synthesis, as far-ranging and ambitious as those to be found in the medieval Summas, would be able to do this, but then only after having absorbed Teilhard de Chardin's two essential contributions arising out of his cosmic and Christian vision: the discovery, on the one hand, of evolution and its laws, developing into a renewed theology of transforming and unifying creation, and, on the other, the rediscovery of the cosmic role of Christ as the savior and recapitulator of the universe, as it was proclaimed by St. Paul and contemplated by the Greek Fathers.

Throughout his life Teilhard de Chardin looked forward to the coming of such a synthesis; he pointed out the direction it would have to take, and, in language that was cumbersome and quite inadequate, he tried himself to build up this structure, or at least those parts of it that appeared to him to be the object of the most serious neglect in the theological climate of his day. "All the world listens attentively to his message," notes Yves Congar, "for, no matter how imperfect it might be on so many points, it is the only one today that sets forth a new cosmological, anthropological and theologico-christological Hexameron to fit

---

[26] This is clear for the texts on the creative union which are much more theological than philosophical. Neither is Le Phénomène Humain (Eng. tr.: The Phenomenon of Man: New York, 1959) an exception; it has a theological purpose, even if its internal constitution and general approach respect the autonomy proper to scientific disciplines.

the dimensions of our new consciousness of the world." And explaining the confusion of many theologians when faced with such an enterprise, he adds: "We have become so accustomed to looking at the realities spoken of by revelation *on their own,* that we seem to lose them when they are set in the framework of the world and its history. It is true that there is much work to be done, but it must be done." [27]

Teilhard de Chardin was not mistaken. It is only by the working out of an all-embracing theology of the created universe in process of convergence and of Christ as the recapitulator that the problems of the spirituality of the Christian in the world, of the reconciliation of the two passions which must drive him on and of the dialogue between the Church and the world can have new light shed upon them. It must be said that, faced with this need, the theological foundation of the conciliar *Constitution on the Church* is not without its disappointments.

A Gospel of Human Conquest

If it is true then—as spiritual experience undoubtedly assures us and as revelation declares while showing us the vast dimensions of the cosmic adventure—that Christ is the center toward whom and in whom the evolution, which human endeavor must lead laboriously, but in freedom, to its end, is now converging, then Christianity can and must be a "gospel of human conquest",[28] without, however, disintegrating into a purely profane humanism. "To attempt all for Christ. To hope all for Christ. *Nihil intentatum.* There you have the true Christian attitude. To divinize is not to destroy, but to create anew. We will never know all that the Incarnation still looks for from the powers of the world. We can never hope enough from the growth of human unity. Lift up your head, Jerusalem. See the immense crowd of those who build and those who search. In the laboratories, in the studios, in the deserts, in the workshops, in the vast social

[27] Y. Congar, in *Mélanges de Lubac,* I (Paris, 1964), pp. 189ff.
[28] *Quelques réflexions sur la conversion du Monde* (1936) = *Oeuvres,* IX, p. 161.

crucible, do you see them, these men who toil? Well then! All that is astir through them in art, science and thought, all that is for you. Come, open your arms and your heart, and like Jesus, your Lord, gather in the torrent, the deluge of the strength that flows in man. Take it to yourself—for, without its baptism, you will droop without desire, like a flower without water; and save it, since without your sun, it will dissipate itself foolishly in sterile growth." [29]

In this incarnational perspective,[30] the fundamental Christian attitudes are enriched by a new dimension, and "a new interpretation of holiness" is seen to be necessary.[31] Some time before his death Teilhard de Chardin recalled his hopes in this direction.[32] But he was never to have the leisure to put it in systematic form. But, at least, many times he had sketched out some of its features, as in this celebrated passage written in 1933:

"To adore, formerly, meant preferring God to things, by referring them back to him and sacrificing them for him. To adore, now, has come to mean pledging oneself body and soul to the creative act, by associating oneself with it, so as to bring the world to its fulfillment by effort and research. Loving one's neighbor formerly meant not defrauding him and binding up his wounds. Charity, from now on, while not ceasing to be imbued with compassion, will find its fulfillment in a life given for the common advance. Being pure formerly meant, in the main, standing aside and preserving oneself from stain. Tomorrow chastity will call, above all, for a sublimation of the powers of the flesh and of all passion. Being detached formerly meant not concerning oneself with things and only taking from them the

---

[29] *Le Milieu Divin = Oeuvres,* IV, pp. 201-02.

[30] "To plunge deeper, so as to emerge and rise above. To share in, so as to raise up. That is the very law of incarnation" (*Quelques réflexions = Oeuvres,* IX, p. 166.

[31] *Le Phénomène spirituel* (1937) = *Oeuvres,* VI (Paris, 1962), p. 136.

[32] "As well as dogmatic christology, the very notion of Christian perfection cries out to be taken up and its meaning thoroughly reexamined", now that "the age-old opposition between earth and heaven has disappeared (or been corrected) into a new formula: To heaven through the fulfillment of the earth": *Recherche, Travail and Adoration* (1955) = *Oeuvres,* IX, p. 289.

least possible. Being detached now means step-by-step moving beyond all truth and beauty by the power of the very love that one bears for them. Being resigned, formerly, could signify a passive acceptance of the present conditions of the universe. Being resigned, now, will be no longer allowed, save to the warrior fainting away in the arms of the angel." [33]

Because attachment to the world has now become attachment to Christ, the spirituality that Teilhard de Chardin described here, far from being an easy way, is always a way of the cross toward the resurrection: a way of painful transformation into the Greater than oneself. To this the life and the work of the man who wanted to be and was "the evangelist of Christ in the universe" [34] bear eloquent testimony.

[33] *Christologie et Evolution* (1933), pp. 11-12.
[34] *Le Pretre* (1918) = *Ecrits*, p. 298.

Christian Duquoc, O.P./*Lyons, France*

Theology
and Spirituality

Religious Culture, Critical Spirit, the Humility of Faith and Ecclesiastical Obedience

Those unfamiliar with the theologi-an's profession would be inclined to think that meditating on the faith, taking the Word of God as the object of one's thinking, must be the royal road to the encounter with God. According to this view, the theologian would be unaware of the problems faced by his contemporaries in their attempt to unify the secular life with the religious life. The theologian's profession would be so congruent with faith that the theologian would not feel the duality that few Christians succeed in overcoming.

This idyllic vision of the theologian's profession is an illusion. It leads a number of priests, seminarians and laymen to demand from reflection on the Word of God, from religious culture, something that they cannot directly provide. Naively imagining that theology is a royal road to the integration of one's life in Christ, and noting that experience does not confirm this hope, they abandon what seems to them to be merely an intellectual profession but not a Christian attitude. They cannot see how all this apparatus of scholarship can serve to mature the Word of God in themselves. They accuse theology of being too abstract, and some, who pride themselves on a bit of spirituality, suspect a secret pride in those who devote themselves too happily to these studies. Such people see in theology the dangerous upsurge of the critical spirit in the very heart of the Church. In short, they accuse it of being useless from a pastoral point of view. The Church needs zealous pastors and obedient laymen, they say, but not bold or supercilious minds. Let us leave others to worry about things that cannot touch the heart. Theology is thus reduced to being either an academic occupation or else the concern of specialists. Having expected too much from it in the way of a contribution to the Christian existence, and disappointed at its ineffectiveness and aridity, people classify it as having nothing to do with "life". It cannot help toward a personal encounter with God, and therefore cannot be integrated either in the life of the individual Christian or in the life of the Church.

All errors spring from impatience. To demand of theology or of any kindred form of religious culture the immediate unity of life in faith betrays a desire that refuses to accept slow progress. The relationship between "religious culture" and spirituality (in the sense in which "spirituality" denotes the lived unity of human existence in faith) is not a direct one. Theology leads to Christ by a roundabout way, and it is from this roundabout way that it draws its strength to reply to the questions that haunt contemporary Christians and that are all rooted in the dichotomy between their secular life and their faith. Merleau-Ponty not long ago spoke in praise of philosophy. It would be useful today to do the same for theology. The two eulogies might well have much in common: both these two disciplines are uncomfortable for those who cultivate them and for societies that do not put them in chains. Some may laugh at this assertion. They will discern here the taste for free investigation undermining our societies. Never having pursued any other form of religious culture but Scholastic theology, never having experienced the risk implicit in any kind of thinking, whether it be secular or religious, they will see here only a verbal concession to the philosophical demon of our time, namely, the inflation of uncertainty and the idolatrous worship of the question.

I am willing to agree that a Scholastic theology can justify its method by its function, but it should not then claim to embody the theological attitude as such. When I say that theology is a profession, I mean that it unites the various dynamisms in man in order to enable them to undertake a certain task. I should add that it is a humane profession. The theologian does not repeat a tradition, like a worker on a production line repeating stereotyped movements. I remember once hearing a high authority define the task of theology as "repeating the words of the Roman pontiffs down to the last detail". That is not a humane profession, and I have too lofty a conception of theology and of the gravity of religious culture in general to humiliate them to that extent. If in the Church it is only a question of repeating, in the literal sense of the word, the pronouncements of the authorities, there is no need for theologians. The theologian loves his profession as the artist does. A profession can be followed only by a free man, not by a robot. I do not deny that there is a need for teachers who simply repeat what they have learned; but I maintain that the Church does not lack such teachers, and that it has a greater need for genuine theologians than for timorous "doctors". To reduce theology to being nothing more than the physical echo of the magisterium is to despise the study of the Word of God; it is to deprive it of what constitutes the glory of a humane profession, namely, responsibility.

Theology is a humane profession, and all religious culture must tend to assume the same kind of responsibility. The theologian has a Christian vocation. Studying the Word of God with passionate enthusiasm (and if he does not he is only one of the teachers referred to above) does not uproot him from the world. On the contrary, what concerns him is the link between the world and the Word. He is not carried away by the Word, like the mystic; and he is not interested in immanence alone, like the philosopher. His field is the tug-of-war between the Word and the world; not the dogmatism unaware of the open rebellion and the awkward question, but precisely this continually renewed tension between a divine Word that pulls man up short, takes hold of him and saves him, and a human world that puts God on trial. It is an uncomfortable spot for the theologian, for he is not so completely on God's side that he can shut his eyes and display once again the faith of Abraham; he cannot heroically sacrifice reason and say: "I believe because it is absurd." Nor is he so completely on man's side that he can regard the divine intervention as null and void. He inhabits that shadowy region where man and the Word meet. He is the ally of the Word that confutes and banishes all pride; and he is the ally of man who kicks against the pricks and will not be imposed upon.

Thus theology is not the royal road to unity between faith and life, as the layman is only too ready to imagine that it is. Like all forms of culture, theology has its critical moment. Consequently it is liable to disappoint the practical man and the pastor who need immediate certainties. The theologian is always a little to one side of the official truths; but not to one side of the Word of God—if that happened, he would no longer have any reason for existing, although it would be rash to assert that such a situation has never arisen at any time in history. He is an unreliable ally for rulers. He may call in question tomorrow the too immediate—and very useful—truths of today. His job is not to justify present practice, but to collate the Word of God and the "signs of the times". However, from security or ambition, he can renounce his calling, become a mere repeater of accepted doctrine, stop defending man and freedom in the Church, and acting as the mouthpiece of the challenge of the Gospel in the world. This does not imply that there is no challenge of the Gospel with regard to the Church. It certainly exists, but the role of the theologian in this conflict is more particularly to ensure that it is heard to spring from the link between man in process of development and the Word of God.

The theological road is not a royal one; it is full of ambushes. The preliminaries to Vatican Council II are enough to remind us of that.

Some people may say that this is identifying the theological attitude with the philosophical attitude. Moreover, they may ask, what interest is there in describing an attitude which can only concern a few specialists? How, without sophistry, can one compare a theology of this sort with the religious culture to which it is desirable that a continually increasing number of laymen should attain? Finally, how can such a critical attitude be reconciled with the humility of faith and ecclesiastical obedience?

First, let us define, in a very simplified way, the difference between the philosophical attitude and the theological attitude. The philosopher is free: the Word of God does not challenge him; it is not the object of his thinking. No magisterium imposes its interpretation on him. The philosopher is independent of any tradition containing a revelation. But this liberty is too fine to be really concrete in the case of the philosopher who is also a Christian. He puts in parentheses what radically affects his position as a man, namely, the Word of God. Not that this liberty is abstract in comparison with the condition of man in modern society. On the contrary, the majority of our contemporaries do not regard the challenge of man by the Word of God as a source of fruitful reflection. The philosopher, even one who believes, to the extent that he is not an unconfessed theologian is infinitely nearer the problems of today. It is true that, as a believer, he occupies an uncomfortable position, since his autonomous reason does not meet the interrogation of faith so as to make it the object of his thinking. This discomfort arises more from his position as a believer than from his philosophical attitude. It seems to me that for the philosopher faith is a formidable obstacle, but as he is not struggling openly with it he surmounts the challenge by putting it into parentheses; or else he becomes a theologian. Thus the freedom of the philosopher is only real insofar as the divine Word does not erupt into the movement of his thought.

Far be it from me to speak ill of philosophers who are practicing Catholics. Yet I am surprised at the imposing number of believers who treat philosophy seriously and at the small number of those with a similar enthusiasm for theology. Is this more or less disguised rejection of theology an instinct to escape? I should not dare to answer this question. Is it easier to pursue an intellectual faith by putting the Word of God in parentheses than by struggling with it? Is it not possible that the philosophical attitude is adopted by the believer in the lucidity of reflection on faith itself? Is it not also possible that the discomfort of the non-believing philosopher is adopted by the theologian who makes it his own while adhering to the Word and its intellectual challenge? Theology would in that case be the unavoidable tension which takes seriously the combat between man and God. It is certainly something else as well, but it must be that, and all the more today when it has to bear witness in the heart of unbelief and serve as a strengthening example to the believer. It can be cautiously asserted that theology alone is capable of hearing clearly the question posed by disbelief in the concrete, historical form of transcendence manifested in Christianity. And it makes this question its own while retaining its faith. The theologian would be denying himself if he hid his faith under a bushel or if he systematically took no account of it. This also means that the theologian is only faithful to his purpose if he maintains a constant dialogue with the philosopher.

The theologian encounters the Word of God by the roundabout way of thinking. It is a way that has an exemplary value, for the subject of this thinking is the dissociation we all experience between faith and life. Theology is only a path to unity if it takes seriously that duality that everyone experiences on different levels.

The Christian, more especially today, feels incapable of attaining any kind of coherence in himself; so many different tasks and thoughts make demands upon him that he fails to see any unifying factor in them. This fragmentation has been described dozens of times. Henceforth he takes seriously the transformation of this world; he takes part in the scientific and cultural adventure. He estimates the worth of political attitudes. He has acquired a taste for earthly tasks. He works with non-Christians, whose economic or political choices he often shares. How does all this fit into his faith? In most cases he does not see. At best, if he does see, the perception is acquired by a rational effort, a sort of exercise in persuasion that has to be continually repeated, since it is continually threatened. Moreover, the effort does not seem to be very effective, for it does not succeed in bringing to life on the level of vital unity, of "sensibility", what he knows by other means must be true. This explains why efforts undertaken to achieve a better religious culture are most often disappointing. If the culture is biblical, it seems far removed from our mentality and for many people it demands too much in the way of previous historical knowledge. If the culture is liturgical, it is liable to turn into archaeology. If it is theological, it deals with problems whose connection with daily life is imperceptible to most of the laity.

This inability to integrate all these many tasks and interests in the faith, this semi-failure of all efforts to achieve a real religious culture, tends to push the crucial questions into the background. One no longer sees where the originality of Christianity lies. All the cultural or political questions to which one devotes oneself can be explained on the purely human plane. One meets only clearly defined problems to which one must give precise answers if one wishes to avoid falling into idealism. One never meets the Christian transcendence. What the Christian believes emotionally or rationally is not experienced, is not verified in his daily life. He becomes distracted, and the decline into indifference often covers nothing but the bitterness of not being able to isolate the specifically Christian. Because it is everywhere, Christianity is no longer anywhere.

All these questions become obsessive. When they grow too pressing one rejects them as wrong thoughts. What is the good of prayer, of the liturgy, of the sacraments? What is the good of the Christian body and its positive laws? What is the good of explicit belief in God, in Jesus Christ, since I can perform my task as a man just as well without this superstructure of dogma, ritual and ecclesiology?

These questions emerge from a situation in which the believer, participating in the present dynamism of civilization or at any rate subject to it, no longer feels the originality of his faith as significant and unifying. This originality is outside his daily task and alien to his sensibility. Perhaps it is rational, perhaps it is only a sociological relic: many Christians no longer know. Faith is no longer vital. If the Christian is still gripped by the passionate desire to believe, he is thoroughly upset by the situation; if he is tortured by the fear of not believing, he closes his eyes and blocks his ears. He wants to know as little as possible about religion so that no question arises. By saving his energy in this way he keeps alive the smoldering fire which exposure to the gale would extinguish completely. He lives with this fear gnawing at his heart. He avoids any kind of confrontation. He feels rather than knows that disbelief would then take hold of him completely. The reaction against any change in the habits of "religion" springs in some people from the biological instinct for self-preservation. What many people feel is not so much the seductiveness of disbelief as simply weariness; they have grown tired of struggling over and over again with something that is never resolved and are glad to enclose themselves in the immediate security of the things around us. Perhaps if there were no questions to bother about one would be happy. Indifference is akin to the carefree attitude of childhood. In days gone by, faith provided this "childhood"; the simplicity of the Gospel allied itself to the spontaneity of life. Today nothing is simple; the education of children, human love, economics, politics—they are all complicated affairs. No doubt we form an idyllic picture of earlier times, but it remains true that they were less complex. Now our heads are bursting and we need rest. One form of disbelief is the relaxation of the troubled mind. We no longer have enough strength, in the purely physical sense of the word, to stand up to the demands of faith and its obscurity. There was a time when religion was "the opium of the people", but it is on the way to becoming a factor that disturbs its equilibrium. It demands too much of man, by leaving too much room for invention and freedom. It makes him feel guilty. To let yourself live, have recourse only to the immediate, not think of the future, refuse to worry—this attitude gives you time to be human. The Christian is out of breath. Everybody accuses him:

non-believers, of being disloyal or hoodwinked; the Gospel, of being responsible and only mediocre. The Christian is stifling, and indifference is a way out. It is not a deliberately chosen disbelief but an instinctive reaction, with little conscious thought about it, provoked by the superhuman effort required to comprehend the Christian purpose in its present complexity and to achieve the unity desired by faith. The Christian existence has become so fraught with problems as to be inhuman.

Does the theological attitude adopt this form of disbelief? It challenges it by revealing in it a disbelief that is unwilling to come into the open. It would like to awaken it to freedom; at present it is only destiny, sociological pressure.

There have always existed beliefs or disbeliefs lived as a sociological destiny; they bear witness to man's antipathy to freedom. In days gone by, sociological belief was far more widespread than disbelief of the same sort. Today things are different. The social extent of the phenomenon provides many people with a rational basis for their religious indifference. Deliberate disbelief has always been and still is confined to a very small number of people, for it demands a withdrawal from immediate worries and an extremely lucid view of the human condition. It has no illusions about the future. As J.-P. Sartre has said: "Atheism is a long and difficult enterprise." And Simone de Beauvoir knows that not to believe is to feel oneself a mortal and to be occupied with the thought of death. Disbelief of this sort is not just a matter of words. Lucid itself, it accuses faith of evading the condition of man. Disbelief seems to be the temptation of the strongest, the accession to true liberty. Not being a refuge in the immediate, it becomes a struggle for man, who has no providence to look after him. Far from being a form of resignation it is action, but action which knows its limits, unless, tired itself of freedom and lucidity, it creates new idols, and becomes an unconfessed faith.

What is the significance of this for theology and religious education? Theology is a roundabout way that can teach us a great deal. It does not claim to unify faith and life with one stroke of a magic wand. Its starting point is the dissociation that everyone notices. It takes seriously its atheistic interpretation, which arises partly from the contemporary decline of religion. This disbelief never ceases to be the object of its reflections at the very same time as the Word of God is the source of its meditation. Freedom in the process of becoming logical atheism, and yet not ceasing to be challenged by God—that is the principal object of present theological research. Contemporary atheism is the most radical challenge that can confront the Church. Generosity alone is not sufficient to overcome it; it must also be understood. It must be understood not simply as an evil—this is the attitude which the mystic would be liable to take—but as human and as a form of interrogation. It has to be understood from inside, so to speak, as far as that can be done. Not that the theologian wishes to reconcile conceptually the questioning of the atheist and the Word of God; he wants to go to the extreme of human questioning because the divine challenge erupts precisely where the spirit of man is on the move. The task of theology today is to awaken the Church to the seriousness of the question of atheism, and to help Christians to overcome this temptation in themselves, not by shutting them up in the ghetto of pious thoughts but by leading them toward a religious culture which, in accordance with each individual's capabilities, will integrate in reflection on the faith the questioning attitude of which atheism is one interpretation. That is how theology will become a force and an example, and an indirect source of spirituality. By striving at its own risk to think out faith, by taking the progress of atheistic thought seriously, it unifies on the level of its own attitude what is most radically dissociated.

Thus the theologian wants to live professionally and enthusiastically the duality which rends every Christian today, namely, on one hand the faith and on the other the absence of God in daily life. He does this by choosing the most radical duality as the object of his thought, and thus unifying in one profession and one branch of learning what is split everywhere else. Yet he does not cease to be torn himself. For him not to be torn, either human questioning would have to stop being atheistic or faith would have to be less obscure. As a profession which may serve as a symbol of a spirituality for difficult times, theology bears witness that if the duality is not overcome and if the absence of God makes us anxious, it is of the nature of the Christian existence to strive toward a unity that is human and not purely mystical. To give up the idea of unity on the human plane would be as good as banishing Christianity from the cultural field altogether. It could no longer be communicated or discussed or thought about. It would cease to be human. The atheist's accusation that man has no use for God would be fully justified. On the other hand, this unity can never be achieved.

At this point it is possible to reply rapidly to the question whether such an attitude does not involve failing in humility of faith and ecclesiastical obedience.

The answer is a simple one. The Christian temptation is the anticipation of unity, impatience for the kingdom. In his eagerness to achieve unity here on earth the Christian tries to nudge forward the slow development of human affairs. He forgets that even if the kingdom is a gift from on high it is nevertheless the perfection of everything human. Thus all things must be allowed to mature. To incorporate them too quickly in the kingdom, or to regard them too impatiently as signs of the kingdom, is to devalue the meaning of all that happens in due time; it is to regard oneself as the sole repository of the human, to claim that God has already offered us the job of ruling the world in righteousness and justice, and that we are the only people capable of working for a future of this sort. The history of the Church bears witness that the attempt to put such claims into practice has always been catastrophic, that is, damaging to the true spirit of the Gospel.

To take every human question seriously, to appreciate every human investigation, even if the question or the investigation is atheistic in tendency, is to give proof of humility, for it means not identifying the Christian with God and not believing oneself exalted by faith to the clear vision of the world that God enjoys.

For the Christian, pride would consist in rejecting the faith because he cannot master it. Humility can allow him great critical daring. He will do the Church far more service by adopting this point of view than by practicing a sheep-like obedience, an obedience that would have him call black white.

What the Church needs in these unbelieving times is free men. Any religious culture worthy of the name must, so far as the individual is capable, make room for the questions posed by our contemporaries. Open to every movement of the mind, it is an advance to freedom. It will only be this to the extent that it aims at producing not just teachers who repeat what they have heard, but men of judgment. It will then teach people how to live with this duality which cannot be overcome here on earth. On a level lower than that of reflective theology it can be instructive, and therefore provide hope, for those who have neither the time nor the means to achieve this education.

Once we have seen where the role of religious education fits in today, we can also see how closely it is intertwined in the Christian existence, and how in practice it even contains a "spirituality". The Christian cannot escape from this world. He has to live with this dichotomy. This personal or collective dichotomy is, so it seems to me, the only situation which corresponds to that of the Church before the Parousia.

Ernest Larkin, O.Carm./*Washington, D.C.*

Asceticism in Modern Life

INTRODUCTION: STATEMENT OF THE PROBLEM

The cross and the resurrection represent the negative and positive poles of death and life in Christian existence. They are correlatives. The evangelical demand of total renunciation (Lk. 14, 26) is the direct and immediate counterpart of the law of total love (Mt. 22, 37). Like poverty of spirit and contemplation in St. John of the Cross, unselfishness and charity are practically the same thing; they exist in direct proportion to each other. Total commitment to Christ is total abnegation of self-centeredness.

Death to the old man and a full life in the Spirit are achieved by the process of asceticism. This human effort under grace is complemented by the passive purifications and mystical graces. In the past asceticism has emphasized the negative pole and devised exercises and observances to chastise the body and bring it into subjection (1 Cor. 9, 27), to mortify the works of the flesh (Gal. 5, 16-21), to suffer with Christ in order to be glorified with him (Rom. 8, 17). Asceticism's task has been one of discipline and control, its purpose the achievement of a dynamic equilibrium or detachment which is the proper disposition for possessing God in contemplative union. St. Teresa of Avila summed up this point of view rather neatly: "When we empty ourselves of all that is creature and rid ourselves of it for the

100

love of God, that same Lord will fill our souls with himself." [1]
Self-denial, renunciation, penance and sacrifice have thus been
the first order of business in a spiritual life dominated by the
cross and oriented to a loving knowledge of God.

Our age has reacted against this type of asceticism as artificial
and opted for a more positive, outgoing, resurrection-centered
spirituality. People today are impatient with a cross separated
from the resurrection, with fabricated penances, but especially
with any device that would separate them from the challenges
and suffering of a full-time, involved life with their fellow human
beings. It is not a matter of being less willing to suffer or to strive,
but rather of accepting the self-denial inherent in a love of God
and this world. "I would like to be able to have a great love for
Christ," wrote one of the clearest spokesmen for this new asceticism, Teilhard de Chardin, "in the very act of loving the universe. . . . Besides union with God and union with the world,
is there not a union with God through the world?" [2] Such a goal
will bring its own brand of asceticism; the asceticism of material
negations and explicit reduction of interests and involvements
will cede the place of honor to one which accepts the unpredictable demands of daily life and duty, the trials and disappointments, the Teilhardian "diminishments" inevitable in the progress
of human life.

This new approach appeals to modern man. Is it viable? Is
it as effective as the old asceticism of frontal attack and strategic
flight? Can the committed Christian of the 20th century find
sanctity without cultivating the silence and withdrawal, the long
formal prayers and spiritual readings, the penances and mortification, all of which were key points in the spiritual life of his
forebears? In a word is the old *ascesis* passé? These are the questions of the present paper.

[1] *Interior Castle,* VII Mansions, ch. 2, n. 7.
[2] H. de Lubac, *La pensée religieuse du Père Teilhard de Chardin*
(Paris: Aubier, 1962), p. 350.

I

BASIC PRINCIPLES

All Christian life is a living of the paschal mystery and consists in the passage from death to life sacramentally expressed, especially in baptism and the holy eucharist, and existentially lived in one's daily life. More concretely, the spiritual life is a process of mortifying egoism and deepening charity. The passage may be characterized by its negative or its positive element, i.e., by a preoccupation with mortification or with growth in virtue.

Theologically speaking, either emphasis is acceptable because mortification implies charity, and acts of virtue are implicit acts of mortification. In other words, Christian asceticism is always and only ordered moral activity. Only inordinate self-love and selfish preferences need be rejected, even when it is a question of total abnegation which is a *sine qua non* for high sanctity. Total abnegation and perfect moral virtue are exact equivalents. Total abnegation does not imply that every natural desire is evil. It accepts willingly ordered loves of earthly values, enthusiastic involvements in human affairs and activities, or the "passionate indifference" of Teilhard de Chardin.

Whether the ascetical effort, therefore, is explicitly abnegation or virtue, it inexorably moves the person to detachment and charity. The Christian's fundamental option is not only an orientation to God but a conversion from inordinate self-love; hence it is equally serviced by negative and positive acts. Proper spiritual direction decides the individual proportion of involvement in the world and withdrawal from it, of the use or the renouncement of human goods. Detachment actually implies a rich love of the world, since it is nothing less than freedom rooted in charity. It is an utter openness to reality and a willingness to respond to whatever call God gives. Each Christian must be totally detached; pride and concupiscence must never get in the way of his service of God. But the detachment can be expressed as much in dedication to building up the earth as flight to the desert. "We at once see," wrote Cardinal Suhard, "on what conditions human endeavor is made possible and legitimate; it is not a question of how much, or of where, but of the spirit." [3]

II

FORMS OF ASCETICISM

The state of perfect detachment and perfect charity is attained only gradually. Heirs of original sin, we enter the world alienated from God and disintegrated within ourselves. As Christians we are redeemed, it is true, and there is "no condemnation for those who are in Christ Jesus" (Rom. 8, 1). But the work of progressive redemption remains. We still experience conflict between the law of God and the law of the members within (cf. Rom. 7) and we still must struggle against enmity toward our neighbor without (cf. Eph. 2, 14); *ascesis* is necessary to achieve integration within and unity without. The work is the Spirit's from beginning to end, but he calls upon our free response and cooperation. The two forms of asceticism are two such responses.

The older form conceives the Christian life in terms of personal transformation rather than service or apostolate. Transformation comes first; service is an addition or effect. This older spirituality is frankly contemplative; it centers the life of the Christian in prayer, i.e., in conversation with God that begins here and continues into eternity. It singles out the otherworldly, transcendent aspects of the mystery of Christ, concerns itself almost exclusively with the individual's relationship with God and not his relationship to his fellowmen or his world and pays scant attention to man's responsibility of building up the new heaven and the new earth. The kingdom of God is a kingdom of souls, whose salvation is the "one thing necessary", the one absolute. All else is relative. Human affairs, for example, or temporal realities have no permanent significance; they are mere

[3] "The Meaning of God," in *The Church Today* (Chicago: Fides, 1953), p. 211.

means, valuable in proportion to their usefulness for the salvation of souls, but in themselves destined for the dust heap.

In this perspective and in view of man's weakness the only logical course of action for the Christian is to consider this world a hazard and pitfall and to flee from it. Tutiorism takes over and counsels withdrawal from earthly concerns lest one be led astray. The practices of mortification aim to neutralize the body's influence; the senses and faculties are denied their proper objects in order to promote better equilibrium and allow for the peaceful search of contemplative union with God. Silence and solitude discourage dissipation and worldliness. Inordinate self-love is ruthlessly sought out in one's every action and directly dealt with either by rejection of the action or by protest; an insurance against inordinate self-love is to seek the difficult rather than the easy, the unappealing instead of the pleasant.

Detachment rather than charity thus directs the ascetical efforts in this system. If God is to be encountered in prayer and religious acts, it behooves a man to purify himself of the profane and prepare his soul for the meeting. This he will do by putting off the old man and putting on the new. This conversion is to be achieved by frustrating his own earth-bound will, refusing his own comfort, searching out the divine element in all his acts. In the past this divine element meant the good intention; a man had to justify his works by the purity of his intention, since this gave the primary spiritual significance to his acts. In short, the spiritual life was a struggle between the two contraries of love of God and (inordinate) self-love. Cancel out the latter and the former will stand revealed in a man's life. The simplicity of this system has much to recommend it, but today one can easily detect its weakness in its neglect of the dimension of the temporal and created.

The new asceticism differs from the old in many ways. Whereas the Christian of yesterday feared egoism and worldliness and tended to seek God outside this world in pure adoration, the Christian of today begins with himself and the world as he finds them and expects to find God there. The resurrected

Christ lives and works now in the community of his followers, and the Christian through his own apostolic activity is caught up with Christ. The spirituality of today is profoundly this-worldly, incarnational, even "religionless" in Bonhoeffer's sense. The world has been corrupted and used for sinful purposes, but it is also a redeemed world, on its way to complete redemption (Rom. 8, 21). There is less concern today about sin in the world than grace for the world, less thought about impure or ambivalent motivation in the Christian than his being an instrument of grace contributing to the extension of the kingdom of Christ on earth. Sin and selfishness continue to be the blocks hindering the progress of the kingdom, but these impediments are eased out by the works of positive charity as effectively as by direct confrontation. Today's Christian looks upon efforts to neutralize or frustrate inordinate love as something outside the main axis of the spiritual endeavor. He is not concerned with purification but with commitment, and for him this means action, work, doing for others. He is very optimistic, sometimes quite presumptuous, in appropriating human motivations and identifying his projects as the work of the Lord. He accepts difficulties; he knows he must rise above ambivalent or selfish feelings and overcome frustrations, ingratitude and the other obstacles to persevering efforts on his part. He thus finds abnegation and suffering in abundance. Self-imposed mortifications seem contrived compared to the unavoidable crosses of the human condition.

This effort is sanctifying in proportion to its virtuous character. It is a valid implementation of the paschal mystery insofar as it is the incarnation of genuine charity. The difference in the new asceticism, in other words, is one of emphasis. The old asceticism fought a rear-guard action and attempted to keep the enemy outside the perimeter, to hunt down and kill infiltrators that had penetrated into one's own lines. The new asceticism is offensive rather than defensive and carries the battle to new fields. It seeks to extend one's own perimeter. It looks outward instead of inward; in fact, the new asceticism suspects introspection, even for the purpose of scrutinizing motives, and thinks introversion is a bad word. The new asceticism teaches a way to God by extroversion, by action. It tends to neglect contemplation, and this is one of its great weaknesses. But while the thrust of Christian love today is concern for the redemption of the world rather than contemplative union with the Lord, the apostle soon realizes that these two goals coincide and that both of them prosper or recede together.

Such, then, are the two asceticisms, described in black and white and hence caricatured to some extent. What is their relative value? Can the second form replace the first as the asceticism of our time? This is the question of the final section.

III

EVALUATION OF THE TWO ASCETICISMS

Vatican Council II reminds us that we must continue to "bear about in our body the dying of Jesus, so that the life of Jesus may also be made manifest in our bodily frame".[4] The Pauline phrase suggests the new asceticism, a putting to death of evil by indirection, i.e., by simply being a good Christian, fulfilling obligations, accepting hardships and responding fully to the leading of the Spirit. Pauline asceticism is the gradual implementation of the exigencies of grace in all areas of a person's life. It is not a technique of neutralizing or deadening lower appetites in man in order to express later a higher activity, but rather a response to the call of God to transcend oneself here and now in an act of love and service. The struggle is between sarkic-psychic man or man without grace and the spiritual or pneumatic man who lives by the Holy Spirit.

The approach we have called the new asceticism is expressly taught in some of the particular decrees. To cite but one example, the *Decree on the Ministry and Life of Priests* presents a

---

[4] *Constitution on the Sacred Liturgy*, n. 12, citing 2 Cor. 4, 10 (Glen Rock, N.J.: Paulist Press, 1964), p. 36.

priestly asceticism of labor and care;[5] priests are encouraged to "cultivate the asceticism proper to a pastor of souls, renouncing their own conveniences, seeking what is profitable for the many and not for themselves".[6]

The main advantage of this kind of asceticism is that it finds God where God chooses to come to us, in the people we meet, the work we do, the secular city we live in. This down-to-earth emphasis precludes an unhealthy emotional withdrawal from the world about us on the plea of spiritual life. One can begin by striving to love nothing but God and end by loving neither the world nor God. This is a hazard of monastic flight or of a fear of attachments that is premature or excessive. In other words, detachment, consciously or unconsciously, can be used as an excuse for apathy to cloak over a selfish refusal to be interested in others or to be involved in human tasks. This, of course, is a bogus spirituality that has received ample criticism in our time.

But there are also hazards in the new asceticism. Perhaps the most obvious one is excessive optimism. Devotees tend to approve all morally justifiable love and use of this world's goods as authentic Christian action, without asking whether the usage or involvement is ordered and according to God's will. "Incarnational" spirituality, as it is sometimes called, thus becomes the excuse for self-indulgence. True incarnational spirituality is actually more demanding than the "eschatological" approach because it demands that the Christian relate positively to all reality as containing its own measure of the mystery of Christ. Intellectual honesty and objectivity as well as a purer love are demanded. Eschatological attitudes can be pragmatic and utilitarian. It is often easier, moreover, to strike out an attraction at one blow than continue to indulge the desire in proper moderation. "The royal road of the cross is no more nor less than the road of human endeavor supernaturally righted and prolonged," said Teilhard de Chardin.[7] However, the point is that

[5] Cf. nn. 5, 6, 12.
[6] Cf. n. 13.
[7] *The Divine Milieu* (New York: Harper & Row, 1960), p. 78.

the supernatural righting and renewal are a real asceticism. Without constant checking a person can be swallowed up by his work or his pleasure, his projects facilely identified as God's will, duties neglected in favor of personal preferences. The new asceticism remains an asceticism because it is the response to graced reality in love and service. It is the way of the cross.

The most positive incarnationist must therefore periodically withdraw, momentarily or at regular intervals, and, figuratively at least, go into the desert where he is face to face with himself and with God. He must reflect, pray, reorient himself. Otherwise he will increase and the Lord decrease. Spiritual exercises like *lectio divina* and acts of voluntary self-denial retain a real if limited and less central place in his life. Some of the old exercises, such as the discipline, can be discarded; others such as fasting need renewal and reformation according to their real meaning and modern conditions. In any case his spiritual life is not structured around the problem of inordinate desires and attachments, precisely because it is oriented to immediate action.

Granting the new asceticism, will it bring the Christian to high sanctity? There seems to be no good reason for limiting its usefulness. A complete transformation must take place, and this total love is won at the price of total abnegation. But the total abnegation need not take the form described by a St. John of the Cross. The Christian saint may well reach the heights in the world and through the world; however, it will be through approaching his life more and more as a service, a dedication and a love to the point where he is totally for the other, for God and his fellowmen, and transcends his very self. Until that point is reached he is serving two masters. (Mt. 6, 24). But in the opinion of many authors today there is no reason why a Christian cannot become totally identified with the one Master through the asceticism of love and service of God in the world.

PART II
BIBLIOGRAPHICAL
SURVEY

Claude J. Geffré, O.P./ *Le Saulchoir, Etiolles, France*

Desacralization and the Spiritual Life

It always seems unreasonable and of doubtful validity to use the expression "new spirituality" when we really mean only a different light thrown by the same Gospel on the existence of the believing Christian. Nevertheless, because of the social and cultural conditions of Christian existence and the new historical situation created for the Church in the world, it is beyond question that we are going through a period of change, contention and insecurity in which the traditional spiritualities in the Church are being questioned.

Some have already tried to trace "the main lines of contemporary spiritual tendencies".[1] Insofar as I am concerned, I am mainly struck by three aspects that recur constantly in what has been written since the Council and which seem to me sufficiently decisive for a certain characterization of present-day Christian life.

1. We have a spirituality in which the *world is accepted*. People want to overcome at all costs the dualism between a "lay" life and a "Christian" life. And so, Christianity appears as a way of controlling one's human situation and as a way of living in this world.

[1] A. M. Besnard, "Tendencies of Contemporary Spirituality," in *Concilium 9: Spirituality in Church and World* (Glen Rock, N.J.: Paulist Press, 1965), pp. 25-44.

2. Contemporary spirituality appears as the spirituality of a "post-religious age of faith".[2] It is a spirituality that is aware—not always without a certain distress—of a shift from the traditional expression of the Christian mystery to the cultural environment of modern man. The Christian will then initiate a critical examination of the false scandals of the faith which may derive from a particular interpretation of the message of revelation, but only to stand more open to the actual demands of the true scandal of the faith.

3. I would like to speak of a spirituality of *anonymous charity*. Steering clear of dogmatism, triumphalism and too facile combinations of Christianity and modern ideologies, the Christian is looking, in his own situation, for ways of serving the world as it is in the name of Christ's love.[3]

---

[2] I take this expression from P. Ricoeur, "La critique de la religion," in *Bulletin du Centre protestant d'études* (June, 1964), p. 6. On this status of the faith in an age of uncertainty, see particularly O. Rabut, *La vérification religieuse* (Paris: Éd. du Cerf, 1964), esp. p. 95: "As faith is a *principle* of light or of spiritual penetration, it is linked to an *initial act* of the mind rather than to conclusions. That is why there is no contradiction between Christian adhesion to the faith, with its value of 'enlightenment', and a suspension of judgment." See also J. B. Metz, "Unbelief as a Theological Problem," in *Concilium 6: The Church and the World* (Glen Rock, N.J.: Paulist Press, 1965), pp. 59-77; I. Goerres, "Incroyance du croyant," in *Signes des temps* 4 (April, 1959); P. Roquelo, "Une foi normalement difficile?" in *Science et Foi* (Paris, 1963), pp. 35-67. One might also read the striking statement by D. Dubarle made at the Semaine des Intellectuels Catholiques of 1965. I only quote these lines: "In his writings St. John of the Cross describes the horror of the night of the spirit through which those who want to pursue their assurance of God to the end must pass. Have no doubt about this: modern humanity, with its own awareness and the irresistible rise of its own powers, with that negative spiritual quality which is freedom, with its science, its mastery and increased possession of nature in view of the mastery and possession of itself—this humanity and its energy are going through nothing else but a vulgarization—or democratization, if I may use this word for European societies—of that night of the spirit mentioned by that 16th-century mystic" (*Dieu aujourd'hui* [Desclée de Brouwer, 1965], p. 35).

[3] I quote this characteristic observation of Y. Congar: "The beacons which God has set alight on the threshold of the century of the atom are called Theresa of Lisieux, Charles de Foucauld, the Little Brothers and Little Sisters, with their parallel at Taizé. . . ." in *Pour une Eglise servante et pauvre* (Paris: Éd. du Cerf), p. 123. On the rejection of a

Because C. Duquoc has already dealt with these last two aspects in a previous article,[4] I shall concentrate on the aspect of "presence in the world" and show that this involves a certain idea about the relations between the *sacred and the profane,* a distinction which as yet is far from clear. I am concerned about this question: How far does the process of desacralization going on in the modern world serve what is truly sacred in our faith, i.e., holiness? To put it another way: Should we oppose this movement of desacralization and again create certain sacred regions in order to plant there the faith of modern man? To give point to this investigation I shall start from two recent studies that are particularly significant for present-day reflection on the Church's presence in this world. They put forward two different historical verdicts on the religious situation in the world; in fact, they demand two different spiritualities, or better, two different "styles" of Christian life in the world.[5]

The End of the Era of Constantine

For several years, in a number of articles, Fr. Chenu has written of the passage of Christianity to a Church which is purely a "presence in the world". He has analyzed this process historically and theologically. He has tried to seek there the ways by which the Gospel is incarnated in time. The more the world

"synthesis" between Christ and the world and on the obedience of love as the basic Christian attitude, see the fine article of H. Urs von Balthasar, "The Gospel as Norm and Test of All Spirituality," in *Concilium* 9: *Spirituality in Church and World* (Glen Rock, N.J.: Paulist Press, 1965), pp. 7-23. One may also consult his small book *Glaubhaft ist nur Liebe* (Einsiedeln, 1963) which provides an excellent introduction to the basic themes which he has developed in his great work, *Herrlichkeit.* Among the finest testimonies to what I call the anonymous character of love, I only refer to *Carnet de route de Jean Ploussard,* texts collected by T. Rey-Mermet, with a preface by Paul-André Lesort (Paris: Éd. du Seuil, 1964) and S. de Beaurecueil, *Nous avons partagé le pain et le sel* (Paris: Éd. du Cerf, 1965).

[4] C. Duquoc, "The Believer and Christian Existence in History," in *Concilium* 9: *Spirituality in Church and World* (Glen Rock, N.J.: Paulist Press, 1965), pp. 127-40.

[5] M.-D. Chenu, *La Parole de Dieu. II: L'Evangile dans le temps* (Paris: Éd. du Cerf, 1964) and J. Daniélou, *L'Oraison problème politique* (Paris: Fayard, 1965).

is itself, the more men will be themselves and the more the Word of God will be itself. The more, also, is the presence of the Word of God then a pure "presence", following the rhythm of that humanization that lies embedded in history. As a true disciple of St. Thomas, Chenu gladly supports the progress of natural and profane forces all through history, and he is of the opinion that this support, far from jeopardizing the domain of grace, ensures its transcendence and richness.

Chenu therefore welcomes the present movement of desacralization and laicization insofar as it compels us through the force of circumstances "to get out of the mental and institutional complex of Christianity". "That the era of Constantine and of Western Christendom are at stake may be a dramatic event, but if this decline is the condition that will lead to a new Christendom, it is a magnificent challenge: it underlies the whole of the Council." [6] It is not a question of a sociological Christianization of the masses, but rather of allowing the Gospel to witness more purely, respecting the autonomous process proper to the world while maintaining the primacy of God's Word over the whole apparatus of cult and institution. "The point is not that the Church should build for itself a Christian world alongside of the 'world', but that it should Christianize the world as it grows, as it is in the process of growing in this extraordinary 20th century." [7]

One senses that the Church's abandonment of past involvements and outdated institutions in order to achieve a "purer" presence in the world as such is going to create a new kind of Christian in the world. Such a Christian will experience this dialectic of the Church's mission in his daily life. He will take certain Christian institutions and certain too heavy-handed aspects of the system with a grain of salt, but only to commit himself to whatever new ways his Christian conscience will dictate. Confronted by these new fields in geography, culture, social life and politics of the modern world, he wants to be a missionary

[6] M.-D. Chenu, *op. cit.*, p. 29.
[7] *Ibid.*, p. 33.

of the Gospel and not "the protector of a civilization that he himself has organized".[8] Beyond the zone of the Church's influence, the layman, with both his feet in the world, will act as a Christian, led by the dictates of his conscience and without necessarily being able to lean on directives from the hierarchy. Duquoc writes that the real vocation of the layman will be to show that "Christianity does not despise the world but lifts it up, consecrates it and fulfills it".[9] In this perspective he will try to discern as "signs of the times" the real progress of the world in regard to humanization, socialization, peaceful relations among men, the rise of conscience in the nations and the development of culture. Chenu sees all these secular values as "toothing stones", a kind of *preparatio evangelica* that will lead to the ultimate destiny of man.[10] Because of his new situation in the world, one can understand that the Christian layman finds himself ill at ease in certain spiritualities of the past that used to insist rather on the "dangerous occasions" of life in the world.[11] He now looks for a spirituality that will integrate his life in a world that has become the main field where he must seek his sanctification.

The Life of Prayer—A Political Problem

If we now turn to the study by J. Daniélou, we observe that he pursues a point of view totally opposed to that of Chenu. Let us take some typical quotations. "The conversion of Constantine made the Gospel accessible to the poor" (p. 12). "The faith can really only take root in a country when it has penetrated its civilization, when there exists a Christendom" (p. 14). "There

[8] *Ibid.*, p. 299. In the same sense I may point to the distinction made by Karl Rahner between the action of the Church and Christian action outside the sphere of the Church's influence (cf. *Mission and Grace* II [London: Sheed & Ward, 1964]).

[9] C. Duquoc, "Signification ecclésiale du laïcat," in *Lumière et Vie* 65 (1963), p. 84.

[10] M.-D. Chenu, "Les signes des temps," in *Nouv. Rev. Théol.* (Jan. 1965), p. 37.

[11] Cf. R. Bultot, *La doctrine du mépris du monde* IV, 1 and 2: "Le XIe siècle" (Paris/Louvain, 1964). See also the symposium, *Le mépris du monde. Problèmes de vie religieuse* (Paris: Éd. du Cerf, 1965).

can be no Christianity for the masses without a Christendom; there lies the choice" (*ibid.*). "In a world threatened by atheism, we must defend the substance of the sacred wherever it is found" (p. 98). While some, following Chenu, rejoice in the Church's abandonment of temporal institutions, Daniélou wants to restore a Christendom. As opposed to those who rejoice in the desacralization of the world (it has even become a slogan), Daniélou insists, in an almost provocative way, on resacralization of the world before it can be sanctified.

Nevertheless, we must take a closer look at this. In essence, what both Chenu and Daniélou want is that the faith should penetrate social and political life. What both reject is an oversimplified separation of the spiritual and the temporal, the sacred and the profane, the Christian element and the political element. However, it is not really a quarrel. On the contrary, it is a dispute about fundamentals. Both authors are haunted by the evangelization of the world, a realistic presence of the Church in the world. But both look at man, the world and its evangelization in a different way because there is a difference in their theology of grace, or, rather, their theology of the incarnation of God's Word in history.

For Chenu, progress in Christian life is brought about "not in order to corner the world 'in favor of' grace through an intellectual or political clericalism, but, on the contrary, in order to promote the natural processes and inherent freedom of this world".[12] But when one reads Daniélou, one sometimes wonders whether he really trusts man and the possibility of a faith that relies only on the Word of God. He has, of course, abandoned the dream of a Christendom as it existed in the Middle Ages, but he wants the faith to have other securities than that of God's Word exclusively. And so, he wants to create a kind of sociological preparation, institute certain zones where the sacred and the religious elements are preserved so that the faith of simple laymen is not left without cultural and social foundations.

There is no doubt that Daniélou touches on a real problem

[12] M.-D. Chenu, *op. cit.*, p. 298.

when he fears that the present evangelical revival, in the sense of making faith a more personal matter, might lead to a "Christian elite", a small nucleus of Christians buried in an atheistic world. (In any case, he especially envisages here Rahner's "Church of the diaspora".) He jumps to the defense of the poor, the simple, the "Christian" countries that are in danger of being sacrificed by the prophets of a pure religion who refuse to allow the faith to decline again into rather mixed religious practices.

One can understand Daniélou's worry. But one may also fear that he is providing arms for those who long for a return to the past, and one would like to see him just as much haunted by the other "poor", the poor of the modern world who feel themselves more and more alienated from the Church insofar as this Church is still compromised by superstitious practices and out-of-date institutions. He champions a Christianity for the masses and he sincerely believes that he is following in the footsteps of Péguy, who defended the Church as the "religion of a people".[13] There is no doubt that the poor are the privileged patrons of the Gospel, that Christianity is not a small sect of the "elect" but a community of both saints and sinners; nor can it be doubted that a "pure" Church with no earthly roots in civilization is a ruinous abstraction for both religion and civilization. But when it is suggested that in order to promote this "popular Christianity" we organize society in such a way that prayer and the Church have a recognized place in this society because of the Church's institutions, and that this place is an official one, then I admit I am not in the least convinced. It may perhaps save this "Christian people" of the old Christendom for a time, but it would hardly be justifiable when one thinks of the means to be used to make the Church more present to the non-evangelized masses of the modern world. By dreaming of a new kind of Christendom, Daniélou despairs too quickly of the inventive power of the Holy Spirit. I agree that this living interpenetration of Church and society is desirable in order that the simple poor may live

[13] J. Daniélou, "Le peuple chrétien selon Péguy," in Etudes (Sept. 1965), pp. 175-86.

this Christianity, but I cannot agree with the author in the means to obtain this result. I think that there are other ways to ensure the presence of the leaven of the Gospel within modern civilization without a resacralization of society's institutions and morals. Moreover, one may ask whether, at the peak of this Christendom, this way of collective and individual sanctification did not too often obscure the real work of evangelization.

Daniélou is also correct when he warns us against the danger of a rather popular conception of pastoral work today, which consists in denouncing the ambiguities of religion in the name of an almost Manichaean purity of faith. But in his generosity he is himself exposed to another danger, that of sacrificing the authenticity of Christianity to its universality. This seems very serious to me, and is, in any case, a false dilemma. He does admit somewhere that he rejects "Churches that would remain sociological remnants of sacred societies where mechanical gestures would continue to be the regular practice" (p. 41). But this does not explain away the fact that he tends to consider as normal a situation in the Church that should be a *border phenomenon,* namely, the fact that there are baptized people who have not been truly evangelized. I find it easier in this regard to follow Hans Urs von Balthasar when he says: "The least one can say here is that a baptismal bond which is not freely and fully accepted at the age of reason by the Christian in question is a wholly obscure enigma for himself and totally incredible and scandalous for others. It is only in such border phenomena of Christendom that one speaks—apparently in the case of the practicing faithful—of the task to bring about a 'synthesis' of Christ and the world, between a Christian existence and an existence that conforms to the world." [14]

Finally, I most strongly disagree with Daniélou about the function of religion and the sacred with regard to faith. In his argument this function cannot be detached from a highly ques-

---

[14] H. Urs von Balthasar, "The Gospel as Norm and Test of All Spirituality in the Church," in *Concilium* 9: *Spirituality in Church and World* (Glen Rock, N.J.: Paulist Press, 1965), pp. 18-19.

tionable historical judgment about the religious growth of mankind and the meaning of contemporary atheism. Basically, the point is whether the world must be "sacralized" before it can be sanctified or whether the present process of desacralization can, in spite of its vast decline in religion, create a new opportunity for an authentic revival of the Christian faith. In a debate of such dimensions no one pretends to see clearly. But when we talk of revaluing the "religious" and the "sacred" as a condition of a living faith, we should at least know what we are talking about when using these terms.

The Sacred and the Profane

Much confusion could undoubtedly be avoided in the present debate about the relations of the Church and the world, of civilization and Christianity, and on the sanctification of the world by the laity if we started with a firm definition of the relations between *the sacred and the profane*. In the latest edition of *Lay People in the World,* Yves Congar writes: "If we were to re-examine today the question of the relations between creation and God's kingdom, we would carry it further to a *critique* of the basic categories of the 'sacred' and the 'profane.' " [15] The fact that certain thinkers like Daniélou interpret the Christian religion as rooted in the sacred character of the world, while others like Chenu see in the process of desacralization the rise of a more genuine Christianity, clearly shows how ambiguous this word "sacred" is.[16] Moreover, the same people who rejoice in the desacralization of the world are the first to entrust the laity with

[15] Y. Congar, *Jalons pour une théologie du laïcat* (Paris: Éd. du Cerf, 1964), p. 652.

[16] On this double attitude toward the sacredness of nature, see the lucid article by A. Jeannière, "L'athéisme aujourd'hui," in *Rev. de l'Action populaire* (June, 1965), pp. 645-60. Among the many studies of this desacralization, I only mention, apart from Chenu's work, H. Urs von Balthasar, *Dieu et l'homme d'aujourd'hui* (Desclée de Brouwer, 1958); E. Borne, *Dieu n'est pas mort* (Paris, 1956); J. Lacroix, *Le sens de l'athéisme moderne* (Tournai/Paris, 1958); A. Dondeyne, *La foi écoute le monde* (Paris, 1964); O. Rabut, *Valeur spirituelle du profane* (Paris: Éd. du Cerf, 1963); *Weltverständnis im Glauben,* ed. J. B. Metz.

the grandiose task of "consecrating the world", and this proves that they do not use the term "sacred" in an equivocal manner.

Our two authors reject a disastrous separation of Christianity from civilization. However, Daniélou dreams of a new kind of sacred civilization while Chenu is glad to see that "whole fields of economic organizations, social relations, international co-existence and cultural values have thus found an autonomy of function and institutional character in a technological civilization".[17]

Does this divergence not spring from the fact that these authors started with a false opposition of the sacred and the profane, as if the consecration of the world excluded respect for its legitimate profane character? Chenu himself does not escape this danger when he begins by defining the "sacred" as "what is put aside".[18] That is why he has certain reservations about the expression "consecration of the world" and prefers to distinguish this from the "construction of the world". He is totally right in not confusing sacralization with sanctity. "The profane ceases to be profane when it becomes sacred, but when it becomes sanctified it remains profane." [19] *The sacredness of faith* in Christ who consecrates all things to God takes nothing away from the profane character of the world. But we may ask whether we should not, on the level of *creation,* assign a place to a sacred element which, far from excluding the profane, demands and provides a basis for it. Through the mystery of creation there is already a *sacred* element at the root that coincides with the "truth" of the world as such in itself. The true religious sacred element is in the nature of a relationship, and that is why it does not jeopardize the solidity and autonomy of the profane. One cannot oppose the sacred to the profane as if they were two things in themselves. They only become two opposite things when one confuses the true religious sacred element with the sacred element of magic or taboo.

[17] M.-D. Chenu, *op. cit.,* p. 252.

[18] M.-D. Chenu, "Consecratio mundi," in *Nouv. Rev. Théol.* (June, 1964), pp. 608-18.

[19] M.-D. Chenu, *art. cit.,* p. 612.

I found some confirmation of what I had already felt in a very illuminating little book by Jacques Grand'Maison.[20] He tries to show that there is a convergence between what a theology of creation tells us of the twofold dimension of the sacred and the profane in all reality and the conclusions reached by human religious sciences on the genuine religious sacred element. One should avoid beginning by a definition of the sacred in terms of separation: "The sacred is not a thing in itself like the profane; it is a relation." That is why we should reject the extremism of those who want to localize the sacred and to place it in separate zones; this would be a return to the magic kind of sacred of the various religions. But one should also avoid the extremism of those who, in order to ensure the profane character of the world, want to keep only the specifically Christian sacred element, the "sacred" of the faith. One must show how the Christian "sacred" is rooted in that original "sacred" of creation, which is precisely the mystery of man and is, as it were, an opening toward the transcendent. Finally—and this seems most important in the present debate about *faith* and *religion*—the criterion of the genuine religious "sacred" lies in its *anthropological value*. One may say that the "sacred" finds its origin in the heart of man, as an opening toward a possible transcendency, a readiness for challenge.

A few lines which sum up the position of J. Grand'Maison are worth mentioning here: "Over against the two first attitudes of taboo and magic, it [the genuine religious 'sacred'] presup-

[20] J. Grand'Maison, *Le monde et le sacré. I, Le sacré*. Coll. Points d'appui (Paris: Éd. Ouvrières, 1966). For a general study of the sacred and the profane, see the following classic studies: M. Eliade, *Traité d'histoire des religions* (Paris: Payot, 1949); *idem, Le sacré et le profane* (Paris: Gallimard, 1965); J. Cazeneuve, *Les rites et la condition humaine* (Paris: P.U.F., 1958); G. van der Leeuw, *La religion dans son essence et ses manifestations* (Paris: Payot, 1948); R. Caillois, *L'homme et le sacré* (Paris: Gallimard, 1962). From the Christian point of view on this problem, see L. Bouyer, *Le rite et l'homme* (Paris: Éd. du Cerf, 1962); J. P. Audet, "Le sacré et le profane: leur situation en Christianisme," in *Nouv. Rev. Théol.* 79 (1957), pp. 33-61; "Le sens actuel du sacré," in *Maison-Dieu* 17 (1949); A. Martimort, "Le sens du sacré," in *Maison-Dieu* 25 (1951), pp. 47-74; B. Haring, *Le sacré et le bien* (Paris: Fleurus, 1963).

poses the earthly condition, even demands it and provides it with
a basis. It establishes a relation of submission, a seeking of communion with a Being or beings on whom man feels he is dependent, both individually and together with all other beings.
This awareness of a total, ontological 'belonging' invites a total
'devotion to' or consecration of man himself, his tasks and the
world that surrounds him. In this way, the 'sacred' is not a
separate reality, a 'thing', or something independent like the
profane, but rather a relationship that is objective, present, co-
extensive with all being, all reality. While it must be distinct
from the profane, it must at the same time invite consecration.
This leads us to a better understanding of the dichotomy of the
sacred and the profane, two constant dimensions of reality that
cannot be opposed because they belong to different levels." [21]

Examining Daniélou's position once again, we realize what a
pity it is that he did not clear up a number of ambiguities in the
notion of the "sacred" before he set out to make "resacralization" the condition of a popular Christianity. He has said some
very pertinent things in his chapter on "Religion and Revelation"
about how necessary it is for the faith to be rooted in the "sacred"
and the "religious". Unfortunately, his "sacred" is rather confused and his "religious" very naturalistic. Hence his astonishing
bias in favor of *paganism,* while it is precisely the pagan religions
that too often seized the genuine sacred element to exploit it
for the sake of a magic or purely ritualistic "sacred" element.
When he writes: "In a world threatened by atheism, we must
first defend the substance of the sacred, wherever it may be
found" (p. 101), I would gladly agree on condition that he
referred to the original sacred element in creation mentioned
above, that is, the truth of man as a mystery of communion with
God and others. But he refers to the ambiguous notion of sacred
as it exists in pagan religions. That is how he comes to look on
a situation as normal in Christianity which in fact unfortunately
occurs only too often, namely, the fact that "in a Christian country many practice Christianity first as a religion before they have

[21] J. Grand'Maison, *op. cit.,* p. 26.

discovered it as a revelation" (p. 101). To me this seems to contradict both the nature of Christianity and the present condition of mankind.

Thus there originates the dream of a neo-paganism of the man of tomorrow, a kind of "springtime of the magicians", as if this cosmic, scientific, sentimental paganism is Christianity's favorite partner for a dialogue. Daniélou is free to think that contemporary atheism represents mankind in its adolescence (p. 36). Nothing is less easy to prove. In any case, instead of going back to an archaic concept of religion as the preliminary condition for the faith, it would be better to face the present process of desacralization as an inevitable element of our modern culture and to seek to understand its meaning for the future of the faith. This was stated clearly by Paul Ricoeur when he said that we belong to the "post-religious age of faith" and that a "certain 'critique' of religion henceforth is part and parcel of the interpretation and reinterpretation of the language of faith".[22]

I do not know what Daniélou means when he says that contemporary atheism is but a transition from yesterday's paganism to that of tomorrow. It is possible that the over-emphasis on reason in this technological age may spark a fresh pursuit of the irrational and the marvelous. But what can we expect from that new cosmic religion that might lead to a Christian renewal? As Jeannière rightly observed: "This appeal to an unknown natural reality, bigger than man, may be found in a periodical like *Planète*. Its success and the way it spreads sufficiently show the power of adaptation of these archaizing forces. Here we have a renewal of superstition, and we should beware of seeing in it a renewal of religion." [23]

Criticism of Religion

Instead of nostalgically dreaming about a religious age that is past or calculating the chances of a new paganism, we would

[22] P. Ricoeur, "La critique de la religion," in *Bulletin du centre protestant d'études* (June, 1964), p. 6.
[23] A. Jeannière, *art. cit.*, p. 653.

do better to give some thought to what the present criticism of religion demands of the faith. Following in the footsteps of Karl Barth and Dietrich Bonhoeffer, many people today talk about the *opposition between faith and religion*.[24] This debate is often rather confused because there is no agreement on what the parties mean by religion to start with. However, the debate is not purely accidental, and it did not spring from purely tactical motives of pastoral work. It is no more accidental than the problem of demythologization of the language of faith. This crisis is part and parcel of our present culture which has had to swallow and digest such formidable dishes as Marx, Nietzsche and Freud—those "three masters of suspiciousness", as Ricoeur calls them—who devoted themselves to a radical attack on the illusions of consciousness. And they only continued what had been started by Feuerbach, "the first to say and see that man lost himself in the absolute, that the absolute in some way causes real substance to evaporate, and that man therefore now has to reassert his own substance and to stop the process of diluting his substance in the 'sacred' ". And Paul Ricoeur adds: "I would like to think with Bonhoeffer and others that henceforth a criticism of religion, fed on Feuerbach and those three masters of suspicion, belongs to modern man's mature faith. In this sense one can say that this atheism that attacks man-made gods is from now on part of any form of faith. And the first thing we must acquire is a critical sense to deal with that religion which has become a mask—a mask of fear, of domination, of hatred. A Marxist criticism of ideology, a Nietzschean criticism of resentment and a Freudian criticism of childhood distress have now become some of the ways along which any meditation on the faith must pass." [25] When in the future we read that "the problem

---

[24] There already exists a vast literature about Bonhoeffer. In French there is R. Marlé, "Un témoin de l'Eglise évangélique: Dietrich Bonhoeffer," in *Rech. sc. rel.* 53 (1965), pp. 44-76; A. Dumas, "Dietrich Bonhoeffer et l'interprétation du Christianisme comme non-religion," in *Arch. de sociol. des religions* 19 (Jan.-June, 1965), pp. 5-29; C. Geffré, "La critique de la religion chez Barth et Bonhoeffer," in *Parole et Mission* 31 (Oct. 1965), pp. 567-83.

[25] P. Ricoeur, *art. cit.,* p. 12.

of tomorrow is not that of atheism",[26] we shall be inclined to think that the author is speaking of an age other than ours.

As far as religion is concerned, it is certain that we live in a different situation from that of the time of Christ. Christ's contemporaries were people that were spontaneously religious-minded. Insofar as religion deprives man of his substance for the sake of something sacred and magic, we may say with Bonhoeffer that religion belongs to mankind's infancy. By the same token, insofar as mankind has reached adulthood, or at least is coming close to it, modern man can be defined as *irreligious*. There is an element of truth in this historical statement. Even if modern man is still far from being adult, and even if the function of "religion" still continues to influence him in ways that differ from those of the great historical religions, it is certain that the whole movement of modern thought tends increasingly to dispossess God of his attributes in order to apply them to man.

And so, even if we must criticize all the ambiguities of a systematic opposition between faith and religion, the fact remains that the question put by Bonhoeffer is a real one when he asks how we should proclaim the God of Jesus Christ to a man who has not been preconditioned by religion: "What can we do that Jesus Christ may be the Lord of those that are irreligious?" [27]

Should we encourage a religious preconditioning in the sense of the superstitions and idolatries of the old pagan religions? Surely not! We can do without this religious archaism. It would go against that very rhythm of history which is the progress of humanization; it would even go against the movement of the Judaeo-Christian faith which is a criticism of religion in the sense of man's self-justification by means of ritual or in the sense of depriving man of his true responsibilities. If the Word of God has to find a point of contact in man in our desacralized civilization, we cannot turn back to sacred elements that are archaic and illusory; rather, we should restore that sense of the

[26] "The problem of tomorrow is not that of atheism but that of the new paganism which is in search of itself" (J. Daniélou, *op. cit.,* p. 99).
[27] D. Bonhoeffer, *Letters and Papers from Prison* (New York, 1962).

original sacred (on the level of creation) mentioned above, that "sacred" reality which coincides with the truth of man as a mystery that makes him stand open to a way of transcending himself. It is not enough to speak of human nature. Through the mystery of creation the truth of man in his profane (Bonhoeffer would say *weltliche*) autonomy coincides with his standing open to the reception of a Word over which he has no control. This *original sacred* element necessarily has an *ethical* dimension. And it is astonishing to see how Daniélou can completely ignore this ethical requirement in his attempt to root faith in religion. That is why an *irreligious* Christianity seems to him much more horrifying than a *sociological* Christianity. Perhaps he is right. The sacred of the Christian faith demands holiness; it concerns the whole of life and implies a moral commitment. That is why, in getting down to the issues, I would think that an atheism with a moral demand is closer to the real substance of Christianity than a superstitious and mystifying theism.

One can plead for a "popular Christianity", a Christianity of the simple and the sinners, but one can in no way plead for a sociological Christianity that would ignore the personal commitment of faith. This would be a repudiation of the specific character of Christianity as "the most favorable place for the discussion about faith and religion".[28] I refuse to admit that the only way to promote a Christianity of the poor is to resign oneself to a too easy falling back on Christianity as a "religion for the people", as if it were a matter of historical fate. This would not do justice to either the power of the Gospel or to the evangelical resources of the poor.

The Opportunity Presented by Desacralization

Now we can look again at our opening question, i.e., does this irreversible process of desacralization offer a new opportunity for the sanctification of man?

The answer is not a simple black or white. It is obvious that

---

[28] P. Ricoeur, "Sciences humaines et conditionnements de la foi," in *Dieu aujourd'hui* (Paris: Desclée de Brouwer, 1965), pp. 141-43.

desacralization is something tragic in the sense that it creates a void from the point of view of "religion". But insofar as it coincides with a radical exposure of the illusions and idolatries of the "religious" consciousness, it may paradoxically serve the sacred element of authentic religion in which the faith must be rooted. In this sense, the conquest of the universe by modern man, and therefore the decline of the sacred, falls in line with the process of desacralization that lies at the heart of our Judaeo-Christian religion. There is therefore no reason to be as pessimistic as some about this decline of religion. If this desacralization develops in the direction of the truth of man—i.e., of autonomy, responsibility for one's life and solidarity with other men—it can help the true religious sense of the real "sacred" as a reality that is a communion and as a toothing stone for the development of that true religious relationship created by faith.

There is no point in turning back. We must announce the Word of God to a humanity that has become autonomous and has stripped bare a certain amount of religious deviations. Will this "irreligious" man be more ready to listen to a Word that reveals new possibilities of existence to him? One should avoid any naive optimism. As Paul Ricoeur has observed, the decline of the sacred in our modern world has been accompanied by a new advance of rationalism (in the strict sense). But this growth in rationalism in turn coincides with an increase of absurdity.[29] Everything becomes "controllable" in our desacralized universe and no mystery is left. Birth and death are no longer sacred realities; births are planned and death is but a "breaking-off", an accident, among the things that are at man's disposal. And since this growth in man's rational approach goes hand in hand with man's growing ability in production, enjoyment and technical transformation of the universe, one can see that the question of *meaning*, of "what for?", is becoming more urgent every day.[30]

---

[29] P. Ricoeur, "Le langage de la foi," in *Bulletin du centre protestant d'études* (June, 1964), p. 20.

[30] P. Ricoeur, *Dieu aujourd'hui*, p. 140.

Therefore, the counterpart of the conquest of the universe is a more vivid sense of the absurdity of the human condition, so often brought out in modern art and literature. One could also point out that the desacralization of nature and the overemphasis on the rational element produce, by way of compensation, a kind of resacralization, but this time the sacred is no longer immediately linked up with nature but rather with the great collective myths of social groups. "Society now becomes the arena for those forces which man sees and feels as sacred. . . . The desacralization of nature is accompanied by a sacralization of society. This is a wholly new experience in human history." [31]

Must we then—under the pretext that, since religious consciousness has been stripped of its mystifications, *inwardness* has become ambiguous as the field where the true sacredness of faith may develop—rely more on this quasi-sacred communion with history, the world of work and progress? I doubt it. Neither this inwardness nor this communion with the modern collective myths of politics and technology induces man to seek a meaningful answer to the question about God. History is too general to be personal and it is too futuristic. What we must restore to its full value is the domain of *human existence* and the possibilities opened up by the encounter with other people. This differs from sheer inwardness with all its dangers of illusion and from a quasi-sacred communion with the group that exposes us to a magic sacredness.

I would therefore be quite ready to accept the formula that "the substance of the sacred must be defended wherever it may be found", on condition that we understand this sacred in the sense of original truth of man as a mystery of receptiveness and communion. Everything that restores man as "sacred history" has preparatory value for the reception of the Word of God. We must return to our origin in order to rediscover in man that soil which is full of receptiveness and stands open to the Other, the soil of freedom, not for the unlimited power to disagree, but

---

[31] J. Ellul, "Le sacré dans le monde moderne," in *Le semeur* 2 (1963), p. 36.

rather the power to love and to give. We must encourage the sense of personal encounter with other persons without turning this encounter into a kind of magic. We must turn this encounter into commitment, recognition of the Other as a mystery of freedom that cannot be violated. In this sense we might read again these words of Hans Urs von Balthasar: "If non-Christians complain that the universe no longer speaks of God today because, it is said, the universe is no longer orientated toward God but toward man as its goal and its meaning, they only have to take the neighbor seriously in the way in which they themselves are taken seriously as neighbors by [true] Christians in order to find the shortest and most convincing way to God." [32]

At a time when God seems useless in a world in which we seek effective control of everything, there is perhaps an opportunity for man to seek God *for himself* and not because of his usefulness. We should not seek God when we have reached the end of our tether in our experiences as a kind of stopgap for our inadequacy or as a solution for problems we cannot solve. We must create in ourselves a "space for being queried" so that we can learn to *wait* for God to call us, for God as an event, as a creative Word that rouses in us new possibilities of existence.[33]

The Borderline of the Distinction between Faith and Religion

In conclusion, if we want to find an answer to the problem of an irreligious Christianity in the sense of Bonhoeffer, I would say that the irreversible process of desacralization which the world experiences today does not encourage the rediscovery of

[32] H. Urs von Balthasar, "Meeting God in Today's World," in *Concilium* 6: *The Church and the World* (Glen Rock, N.J.: Paulist Press, 1965), pp. 35-36.

[33] In this way Ricoeur tries to get beyond the Freudian criticism of religion in his book *De l'interprétation. Essai sur Freud* (Paris: Éd. du Seuil, 1965). The author thinks that the demystification, which has become inevitable because of this cultural development of psychoanalysis, is the very task that faith must undertake. For a theological appreciation of this study of Ricoeur's, see the excellent chronicle of J. Pohier, "Au nom du Père . . ." in *Esprit* (March, 1966), pp. 480-500, and *Esprit* (April, 1966), pp. 947-70.

the specifically Christian religious element insofar as it is of the very essence of the Christian faith to try to overcome the gap between the sacred and the profane common to all religions. Faith is an act that involves man's whole existence leaving nothing profane or neutral from the moral point of view. As we have seen already, there is therefore room for a *criticism of religion* which is not only legitimate but is demanded by faith and sanctity insofar as religion means an attempt at self-justification or a refusal to accept responsibility for one's own life. But if by "a-religious Christianity" we mean to deny that faith is rooted in a religious dimension of man and necessarily will express itself in a religious manner, we are faced with a deadlock.

The Christian faith, indeed, is the faith of man *in his human condition*. It is rooted in that original sacred element that is the truth of man as God's creature. Without his knowing it, God is the very horizon that dominates his existence and his encounter with other people on the personal level. On the other hand, the hearing of the Word of God, the reception of the sacramental signs by which the Lord has chosen to commune with us, the prayer that man addresses to his God in adoration, thanksgiving and demand for his assistance—all these are human expressions that are bound to have a religious character. *Prayer,* particularly, is a decisive criterion by which to unmask all the ambiguities that lurk behind the question of an "a-religious Christianity".[34] In other words, Christianity is not "pure faith"; it is the true religion because it is man's response to the true God. Faith does not oust religion, but takes hold of it and sanctifies it. It compels man to purify all religious manifestations that may tempt him to seek his own justice.

Several times in the course of this discussion I have pointed out the dangers of a sociological Christianity that would dispense man from committing himself personally, and of a too facile religious Christianity that would dispense man from courageously taking responsibility for his human existence. God must

[34] Cf. J. Bosc, "Note sur Foi chrétienne et religion," in *Parole et Mission* 31 (Oct. 1965), pp. 584-89.

be seen at the center of our life and not on the boundary where we reach the end of our tether. But we should not, under the pretext that modern man has become adult or believes he has, preach an "a-religious Christianity" which has made up its mind that man is *self-sufficient*. Faith as man's response to the true God creates the true religious relationship with God. And whatever phase our human culture may go through, faith will always demand a trusting surrender to God. But the true believer knows that this surrender is never a rejection of responsibility or an alienation. The strange truth is that man can only find himself by losing himself and transcending himself in him who is his life, his freedom and his happiness.

Baldomero Jiménez-Duque/*Avila, Spain*

Current Spanish Literature on Spirituality

Literature concerning the problems of the spiritual life is again becoming important in Spain. In earlier centuries, of course, the spiritual life—whether as something directly experienced and expressed, or constructed as a theory on more or less strict Scholastic patterns, or as "devotion" and vulgarization—had an enormous wealth and diversity of literature. The output collapsed during the 18th and 19th centuries, with the exception of a few prophetic figures who appeared in the last century.

The reawakening came in the first half of this century, but its extent was very limited. Writers looked for links with the 17th century and took up the arguments as to where and how they had been left by the quietist crisis. On the basis of certain more or less questionable theological principles, and others derived from rational and abstract psychology, debates ranged widely and often bitterly around a few questions whose validity was considered *a priori* established: whether or not contemplation can be acquired; whether or not the call to mysticism is universal; whether perfection in sanctity is possible without mystical experience, or with it, and so on. Mystical experience, with certain shades of difference, always meant the action of God in the hearts of men. The Jesuits Villada and Seisdedos, the Dominican Arintero and the Carmelite Crisógono de Jesús were the names most in evidence in the discussion. The illustrious Amor Ruibal who asked the really important questions about spirituality— not merely from an historical point of view, but philosophical and theological as well—especially deserves honorable mention, even though his philosophical studies led to no positive and definite conclusion.

Now the position is very different. Spanish spiritual writing rapidly adapted itself to the prevailing currents with the powerful stimulus of Vatican Council II, even though perhaps a little late and under the influence of numerous translations of foreign works.

In this survey I propose to limit myself to original and worthwhile Spanish works, grouping them into the five categories that seem to be most interesting, excluding purely historical works, which grow constantly better and more numerous, and new editions of ancient texts, also naturally a particularly abundant genre in view of the immense riches of spiritual life and literature in Spain in past times. A bibliography of modern literature on such universally admired figures as Ramon Llull, St. Ignatius of Loyola, St. Teresa of Avila and St. John of the Cross would alone fill several volumes.

The passionate quest for the eternal, the absolute, has been a constant feature of the Spanish mind. The problem of religion has always been in the forefront and has permeated Spanish culture. Moreover, since historical circumstances meant that from the 15th to the 19th century the only "religion" of practical consequence was Roman Catholic Christianity, the expressions of this quest were either intensely Catholic or, by reaction, furiously anti-Catholic. This is undoubtedly the basic and underlying debate in all Spanish culture and letters.

The modern version of this passionate quest for the eternal —ultimately, for God—has been given form by Miguel de Unamuno (principally in *Del Sentimiento trágico de la Vida*). His case might be called archetypal in this respect, and his impact on large sectors of Spanish culture has been enormous. He not only poses the problem of God in elemental terms, but, by the strength of his feeling and his "existentialism of the heart", he raises his fascinating inquietude and uncertain solution—his hope-in-despair, one might call it—to mystical heights. The line that he traced out has been followed with either orthodox feeling or original depth in works such as *Naturaleza, Historia y Dios* by X. Zubiri (Madrid, 1944), *Catolicismo y Protestantismo como formas de existencia* by José-Luis Aranguren (Madrid, 1952), *La espera y la esperanza* (Waiting and Hoping) by Pedro Laín Entralgo (Madrid, 1956), *Razón Teológica y experiencia mística: En torno a la mística de S. Juan de la Cruz* by A. Ortega (Madrid, 1944), *Teología para universitarios* by M. Benzo (Madrid, 1961) and others. In these, zones of spirituality and "religion" in the Christian sense meet and intermingle, with the aim set at the distant horizons of perfection.

Man's discovery of God is not the end of a dialectical, rationalistic process. It is a vital intuition and hence also rational. This is where the mystery lies. Then, if you like, comes the dialectic, arguing around the mystery, which has now become a problem. And the reencounter with God takes place in the measure that man's heart is opened to the revelation which faith can perceive and charity turn into a living experience. Metaphysical experience is thus prolonged in mystical experience, and it becomes "the integral experience" that Bergson saw in the great Christian mystics. This is the line taken by O. González de Cardedal in *Teología y Antropología: El hombre imagen de Dios en el pensamiento de Sto. Tomás* (Madrid, 1956). According to St. Thomas, man, the effect and image of God, can be explained and reach the possible fullness of his perfection in God alone. St. Thomas develops these concepts from their more or less complete expression in numerous earlier Christian writers.

The view of man as he is, as today he comes to know himself better, and so as he practices his religious life, or, even more, as God seems to recreate it in each man, is producing a series of works that apply psychological methods to the phenomenology of the spiritual life over the whole range of its possibilities and varieties. The approach is existentialist, based on scientific psychology, not abstractions, avoiding the tendency to particular, individualistic descriptiveness which has tended to characterize Spanish spiritual writing since the 16th century. Typical of the new approach are *Psicoanálisis y dirección espiritual* by C. Vaca (Madrid, 1952), *Introducción a la ascética diferencial* by A. Roldán (Madrid, 1960), and numerous articles such as "Las anomalías psíquicas en la dirección espiritual" by José-María Poveda Ariño, in *Revista de Espiritualidad* 94 (1965), and "Contribución a la dirección espiritual del psicópata" by J. Antonio del Val in nn. 83 and 84 of the same Review (1962).

Vatican Council II's solemn endorsement of the advancement of the laity in the Church is reflected in many works seeking to define the perfection of Christian life in a form suitable for the lay people who make up the majority of the holy People of God. Spiritual literature in general had of course suffered from being conceived for those who had renounced the temporal implications of human life, or who at least tried to withdraw themselves as far as possible from them. The monastic state had come to be seen as the *analogatum princeps* of perfection in sanctity.

Now the increasing depth of studies of the mystery of the Church and the various secular institutes that have sprung up over the past hundred years have reawakened consciousness of the fact that all the baptized are called to perfection. There are many books testifying to this. *En tierra extraña* (In a Foreign Land) by Lili Alvárez (Madrid, 1956), a challenging and enjoyable book, is constantly being reprinted. It is a manifesto and a work of documentation at the same time, lively in the extreme. *Ascética del hombre de la calle* (Ascetics for the Man in the Street) by Luis de Echevarría (Barcelona, 1954), *El valor divino de lo humano* by J. Urteaga (Madrid, 1956), *Hombre y mujer* (Man and Woman) by José-María Cabodevilla (Madrid, 1960), *La espiritualidad seglar* by A. Huerga (Barcelona 1964) and *Oración y vida del laicado actual* (Prayer and the Life of the Laity Today) by J. Ordoñez Márquez are all excellent examples of this growing genre of works expressing the aspirations and desires of the laity. The Review *Apostolado laical* (The Lay Apostolate), among others, continually keeps the topic alive.

The particular theme of holiness in marriage, one of the most expressive situations of the lay state, which Cabodevilla's book touches on, is producing a whole spate of literature of varied quality. *Mística para seglares* (Bilbao, 1963) by F. Pagés Vidal, is a profound study of lay spirituality. Several Theology Weeks at the Instituto Francisco Juárez have been devoted to the problems of marriage. The present writer has just launched a serious theological work on the same subject, *Santidad y vida seglar* (Salamanca, 1965), in which lay spirituality is considered simply as synonymous with Christian spirituality.

This is self-explanatory, since it is baptism that makes man a Christian "person", a "person" in the Church. His ethic of commitment to Christ is that of the beatitudes. They oblige him to live in a state of eschatological and transcendent tension, the state of a pilgrim in the midst of temporal realities, incarnate in them for the purpose of redeeming them and consecrating them with his Christian inspiration. He lives in a state of inevitable ascesis which his condition of sinner and his communion with the mystery of Christ require of him continually till the end of his life so that he may merit heaven and the glorious resurrection. The types of spirituality proper to those who are not laymen (monks, clerics, etc.) then need to be defined with their own specific characteristics according to their ontological and juridical position among the People of God. It is not the layman who should be defined negatively, as a non-cleric, but the cleric who has to be defined as a non-layman, or, more properly, as a layman with certain qualifications.

The main need is to simplify the largely artificial problem of different "spiritualities" with Christianity. The basic mystery is the same for all; its existential realization is personal and unique to each one of us; the variations required by charisms of function (for the better functioning of the Church) between different "orders" or groups of the baptized are the only ones that allow us

to talk of distinct spiritualities with any theological justification
—a plurality of spiritualities of one and the same spirituality.

On the subject of priestly spirituality *Espiritualidad del sacer-
dote diocesano* by J. Capmany (Barcelona, 1962) deserves mention. There are also numerous articles and symposia, such as the
volume *Homo Dei* (Vitoria, 1962) on the subject. The first volume of *Studia Monastica* (1959) by G. Colombás deals with
monastic spirituality, as does another article by the same writer,
"The Concept of the Monk and Monastic Life up to the End
of the 5th Century," in *Paraíso y vida angélica: Sentido esca-
tológico de la vocación cristiana* (Montserrat, 1958). F. Sebas-
tián Aguilar's *La vida de perfección en la Iglesia* (The Life of
Perfection in the Church) (Madrid, 1963) has aroused a lot of
discussion. There is also interesting material in the four volumes
of *Acts of the Congress of Perfection and the Apostolate,* held in
Madrid in 1956.

Even before the Council, this renewed attention to the mystery of the Church, with its implications, has led in Spain, as
elsewhere, to a reawakening of a spirituality with a strong communal and social spirit, replacing the individualism and devotionalism predominant in the Renaissance, Baroque and Roman-
tic periods of Western culture. (Not that this individualism and
devotionalism were always empty of meaning, it must be admitted; they often led to a rich outpouring of brotherly love.)

Among more general works with valuable comments on this
theme are *S. Pablo, maestro de la vida espiritual, o la ascética
de S. Pablo* by José-María Bover (Barcelona, 1952), *El cuerpo
místico de Cristo* by E. Sauras (Madrid, 1952), *La Iglesia. Misterio y Mision* by A. A. Galve (Madrid, 1963), *La Iglesia misterio de comunión* by A. Bandera (Salamanca 1965), *El misterio de Cristo. Introducción dogmática a la vida espiritual* by
J. A. Segarra (Madrid, 1964), and the proceedings of Theology
Weeks, such as *Teología del laicado* (Madrid, 1954), *El movi-
miento ecuménico* (1953), etc.

More relevant here are studies of liturgy and spirituality,
whose correlation is one of the vital points at which this spiritual-

ity of ecclesial witness receives its highest expression. They have an old but most valuable predecessor, unique in its day, which never received the attention it deserved: *El valor educativo de la liturgia católica* by Cardinal Goma (Barcelona, 1918). Recent publications are: *La parroquia, comunidad eucarística* by Casiano Floristán (Eng. tr.: *The Parish,* Notre Dame, Ind.: Fides, 1964), *La presencia de la obra redentora en el misterio del culto* (The Presence of the Work of Redemption in the Mystery of the Liturgy) by I. Oñatibia (Vitoria, 1954), *Liturgia y espiritualidad* by G. M. Brassó (Montserrat, 1956), *Liturgia y vida cristiana* by J. A. Pascal (Madrid, 1962), and, particularly rich in broad cultural background, *El sentido religioso de la liturgia* by C. Castro Cubells (Madrid, 1964). There are also numerous commentaries on the *Constitution on the Sacred Liturgy* of Vatican Council II, such as the symposium in the Biblioteca de Autores Cristianos, *Comentarios a la constitución sobre la Sagrada Liturgia* (Madrid, 1964), and *Comentario a la constitución litúrgica del Vaticano II* by M. Nicolau (Madrid, 1964). But there is still not a definitive work on the vital interrelationship between persons and community in the religious life of the Christian which the liturgy activates and shows in action. The conclusions of these authors cannot be called original, but they put forward suggestions of varying interest.

The spirituality of the Church is now being fully studied in the commentaries on the *Dogmatic Constitution on the Church* that are continually appearing. There is a recently published symposium in the *Biblioteca de Autoures Cristianos,* in which the essay by the present writer on Chapter V of the Constitution deals with this question in particular. Volume 12 of the Revista Salmanticensis (1965) is devoted to it, and there is a remarkable volume of *Teología Espiritual* devoted entirely to the conciliar themes, with relevant chapters by M. Llamera, "Ascesis cristiano y humanismo"; R. Ortuño, "La liturgia, fuente de la vida espiritual"; B. Monsegú, "Espiritualidad seglar," etc.

I do not propose here to deal with particular themes much beloved of Spaniards, such as the doctrine and practice of the

Spiritual Exercises of St. Ignatius of Loyola (good books constantly appear, such as those by Casanovas, Calveras, Iparraguirre, González, Hernández, Morta). I want to examine only those theological works that produce a synthesis, and more particularly those dealing with the perfection of Christian holiness whose inspiration is more strictly theological.

Recent publications on the subject are *Guiones para un cursillo práctico de dirección espiritual* (Guidelines for a Practical Short Course of Spiritual Direction) by E. Hernández (Comillas, 1954), *Lecciones esquemáticas de espiritualidad* (Schematic Lessons in Spirituality) by V. M. Balirach (Santander, 1960) and *Teología de la Perfección Cristiana* by A. Royo Marín (Madrid, 1954). All follow the classical, neo-Scholastic, ascetic pattern in which the economy of Christian perfection has usually been presented in these last decades. The last-mentioned book has had an extraordinary success. They all adopt a definite and rigid posture in disputed scholastic questions, with no easy concessions to "the enemy". This is largely a consequence of the methods they follow. *La vida teologal* by G. Suárez (Madrid, 1963) is a book of great doctrinal solidity, but perhaps too densely written, which makes it less attractive than it deserves to be.

Among studies of particular questions, the article "Persona y Gracia" by J. Alfaro, in *Gregorianum 61* (1960) deserves mention for its solid theological basis and balance; its theme is the relationship between Christian spirituality and the humanism based on it. There is an article on the indwelling of the Holy Spirit in the soul of the just man by T. Urdánoz in *Rev. Esp. teol.* 6 (1946); on the causal influence of the divine Persons and the mystic experience by B. Aperribay in *Verdad y Vida* 25 (1949); on the sacrament of baptism (theological and kerygmatic reflections), and on confirmation, the sacrament of the Holy Spirit, by A. de Villalmonte in *Naturaleza y Gracia 8* (1961); the spiritual life as progressive participation in the resurrection of Christ by E. M. Mendizábal in *Gregorianum 34* (1953); the causal relation between created and uncreated grace in St.

Thomas Aquinas by J. M. Alonso in *Rev. Esp. teol. 6* (1946); the supernatural life and the action of the Holy Spirit by M. Llamera in *Rev. Esp. teol. 7* (1947), etc. The list could be prolonged almost indefinitely. All these articles are built on biblical and patristic theological criteria, while making wide use of the theological systems of the Middle Ages, with sound historic sense and leading to positive and penetrating conclusions.

Misterio trinitario y existencia humana, a powerful work by O. González de Cardedal (Madrid, 1966), is basically an historical study of St. Bonaventure, but the author draws and enlarges on doctrinal conclusions which make his book an important doctrinal work, a splendid basis for the construction of a truly trinitarian theology of spirituality such as Christian life in fact requires as its point of departure and its destiny and consummation, passing always through Christ. *La experiencia mística de la inhabitación* (The Mystic Experience of Indwelling) by A. García Evangelista (Madrid, 1966), is also indispensable for the study of trinitarian mysticism, rich in theological data and drawing important conclusions.

The present writer, in his *Teología de la Mística* (Madrid, 1963), has attempted to outline a theology of Christian perfection centered on the mystery of Christ and mystically achieved in him, starting from the human condition in its naturally limited and deficient being, but, in fact, existentially immersed in a supernatural climate, of revelation of faith, of divinizing mystery—by, with and in Jesus Christ, which implies a biblical, liturgical and patristic foundation, without forgetting the best theologians or the experiential and psychological witnesses to the mystic life that we are trying to explain. It is the vital intensity of this human encounter with God (with the Father through the Word made flesh in the Holy Spirit) on the different planes that exist in the Church that dynamically constitutes the perfection of holiness—mysticism reaching out toward total oneness with God. For example, the book contains a special study of the relationship between contemplation and action, since their meeting point is a vital one for the study of the supernatural psychology of the Christian striving for perfection.

For the future, there are indications that studies of spirituality will continue on a high level in Spain: the Institute of Spirituality at the Pontifical University of Salamanca organizes Congresses and Study Weeks and publishes their proceedings, as does that of the Discalced Carmelites and the Sainz Rodríguez Center for Historical Studies of Spirituality in Madrid. There are many specialist journals devoted to the subject—*La Vida Sobrenatural, Teología Espiritual, Revista de Espiritualidad, El Monte Carmelo, Manresa, Revista de Espiritualidad Agustiniana,* etc. The late Prof. Sala Balst and the present writer have edited *La Perfección Christiana (Doctrina e historia)*, the first three large volumes of which will shortly appear (published in Barcelona by J. Flors), a further indication of the promise that is increasingly being fulfilled.

Elmer O'Brien, S.J. /Montreal, Canada

English Culture and Spirituality

E nglish of late is less a language in which spiritual books are written than a language into which spiritual books—chiefly French or German in origin—are assiduously translated. Both loss and gain, paradoxically enough, result thereby for the English reader.

The gain is obvious. By the very nature of things the English reader is provided a spirituality which is not enclosed and compressed within the necessarily limited perspectives and experiences of his own culture. Moreover, when one adverts to the exceptional quality of those works which have consistently proved most popular when put into English dress, an additional profit becomes immediately manifest; for who would not be made immeasurably the richer by being made able to read the chief spiritual writings of Guardini, Daniélou, Voillaume, von Balthasar or either of the Rahners?

If less obvious, the loss which is sustained is no less real than the gain. Such works, naturally, do not speak directly to the condition of the English reader—not to his temperament, not to his milieu, not (to put it most bluntly) to his need. There is, in other words, a hiatus between what he learns and how, in his circumstances, he is to live it. And usually he proceeds to close the hiatus in one or other equally unfortunate fashion: he lives what he learns solely within the limits of his head and he ends up a gnostic born out of due time, or else he shapes his behavior to conform it with patterns which are alien to him and so becomes, incongruously, a stranger in his own house.

For both good and ill, a lack of proportion exists in present-day English between translated and original spiritual writing. Because the debits and credits, the loss and the gain, pretty much balance off, there seems little reason to make an issue of the thing. Yet to direct attention at this point to the apparent reason for this lack of proportion could well help to ease the reader's progress through the bookish tangle of the following pages. Therefore, let it be said that the reason, so far as one can judge, is simply the large lack of theologians writing in English.

The interest which theology has come to have for the English reader these past few decades has made him critical of and generally unresponsive to spiritual books that are not manifestly theological. For such books to be manifestly theological, normally they have to be written by theologians. Hence the wide preference for works in translation from the Continent, where theologians appear particularly to thrive. Of course, one would not dare deny that there may well be many mute, inglorious, theological Miltons lurking about in English-speaking lands. But since they are mute, they modify this particular situation not at all.

It need not have been like this. Early in the present century it seemed that it would not be. Who in reading at that time the writings of Columba Marmion and Anscar Vonier would have dreamt that there would be such a subsequent falling away from a tradition of theological spirituality so nobly and comprehensively established?

"Comprehensive" is surely the word for Marmion.[1] He sees the Christian not as an isolated monad, but as a child of God through baptism who lives in imitation of the life of Christ,[2] most

---

[1] It is true that by far the majority of Marmion's works appeared initially in French. However, he was an Irishman, and everyone knows that an Irishman remains an Irishman no matter where he lives or what language he uses. Accordingly, I feel no embarrassment at including him here.

[2] *Christ, the Life of the Soul* (St. Louis, 1922).

fundamentally by making the mysteries of Christ his own.[3] The theological perspective he offers the reader is one that is made real on every page by his constant recourse to the riches of the liturgy and the bible. Ironically enough, it is his recourse to the bible which tends to put off the reader today, and his practice of providing the Latin as well as the vernacular version of the biblical texts is now found to be an unnecessary and irritating distraction. Yet this practice provides a valuable clue to his attitude toward scripture. Scripture is something he has long made his own and long ruminated on *in the form in which it came to him,* the Latin of the liturgy. Scripture is therefore more closely present and alive for him, with consequent benefit to the reader, than a more scientific attitude might have allowed.

While Dom Marmion was a "monastic" theologian in the noble tradition of St. Bernard, Dom Vonier was a "Scholastic" theologian in the equally noble tradition of St. Thomas. However, he was a Scholastic of so liberal a sort that his writings persist in being popular today when Scholasticism itself enjoys precious little popularity. He was, of course, much in advance of his time in the theological emphases he provided, and that precocity has helped. It is a happy commonplace at present that one seeks understanding of one's spiritual situation in the light of ecclesiology, that one strives to see oneself in the total social context of the Church's life. In this sort of thing Vonier proved himself a pioneer. The same can be said of what he wrote about the Church as the People of God and about the centrality of the liturgy, particularly of the eucharistic celebration, in Christian living.[4]

[3] *Christ in His Mysteries* (St. Louis, 1924).

[4] The chief writings of Anscar Vonier have been made commodiously available in the posthumously-edited *The Collected Works* (Westminster, Md., 1952). Volume I, "The Incarnation and the Redemption," includes a shortened version of *The Christian Mind* as well as *The Personality of Christ, The Victory of Christ* and *The Divine Motherhood;* Volume II, "The Church and the Sacraments," contains *The Spirit and the Bride, The People of God* and *A Key to the Doctrine of the Eucharist;* Volume III, "The Soul and the Spiritual Life," includes *Christianus, The Human Soul* and *Life of the World To Come.*

Despite the good example set for them by Marmion and Vonier, theologians in the immediately succeeding decades allowed the writing of spiritual books to fall into other hands by default.

Superficially, Alban Goodier seemed to continue the Marmion tradition. Recourse to scripture, at least in his larger works, was as constant as in Marmion's, but for Goodier it was in the cause of moralizing rather than theologizing. That the moralizing was of an exceedingly high order is something to be grateful for, but it lacks the substance and the continued relevance which only an alert theology seems ever able to provide. However, esteem for the better should not lead one to contemn the good. Particularly in *The Public Life of Our Lord* [5] and *The Passion and Death of Our Lord*, [6] his doctrine is of a singular richness. He almost invariably sets the New Testament texts he invokes against the wide panorama of Old Testament texts and the resultant gain in depth of comprehension is remarkable. If in his larger works Archbishop Goodier was, consciously or unconsciously, the imitator of Marmion, in one small work—his best—he was the innovator. I have in mind *A More Excellent Way*. [7] In this small pamphlet, with a calm which bred general conviction, he replaced the prevalent pattern of spiritual advice (overly given to inculcating methods, multiple devotions, "an everlasting pecking at the soul") with a one-part program of dedication to Christ. The personalist and liberative implications of 2 Cor. 5, 14 have rarely been so persuasively expressed since St. Paul.

Among the many who submitted to this gentle persuasion, I am tempted to include Daniel Considine because the temper of his mind was, in this at least, so similar to Goodier's; however, the chronology of their contributions is none too clear. In Considine's remarkable *Words of Encouragement*, [8] the Christian

[5] Two volumes: New York, 1930.
[6] New York, 1933.
[7] Bombay, no date; Roehampton, 1920.
[8] London, 1927; *More Words of Encouragement* (London, 1929);

life is centered not upon the Christian but upon Christ. For Goodier, it is centered upon Christ as the repository of that love which is to inform and give life to whatever the Christian does. For Considine, it is centered upon Christ as the sole stability possible to the Christian. Moreover, just as Goodier's pamphlet not merely has words about the love of Christ but is filled with it, so is this equally true of Considine's pamphlet in respect to Christian hope; it is one of the happiest and most vitalizing small books that one could possibly read in any language.

What have proved to be the most popular works of Edward Leen and Eugene Boylan, whatever their undeniable merits, are not in this liberative tradition. Leen's *Progress through Mental Prayer*[9] and Boylan's *Difficulties in Mental Prayer*[10] have not unreasonably been felt by some to be excessively devoted to inculcating methods and "an everlasting pecking at the soul". Certainly an unduly large number have discovered new difficulties in mental prayer under Fr. Boylan's tutelage.

Some have also discovered new difficulties under the tutelage of R. H. J. Steuart, but for a different reason. Fr. Steuart's unusually literate and gracious volumes[11] are concerned for the most part with mystical prayer; this can result in an unseemly stretching and straining by the non-mystic who reads them and thereby cause him new and unnecessary difficulties. Yet such a non-mystic, whose name apparently is legion, can profit as greatly from reading Steuart as he can from reading the mystics themselves; he can learn, if nothing else, a new and precious delicacy in his dealings with God.

Prayer was also the common burden of the conferences of

Further Words of Encouragement (London, 1931); one-volume edition, *Words of Encouragement* (London, 1936). It is a compilation of his conferences and letters edited by F. C. Devas, whose own *What Law and Letter Kill* (London, 1953), is in the same tradition.

[9] New York, 1935.

[10] Westminster, Md., 1943.

[11] For example, *The Inward Vision* (New York, 1929); *Temples of Eternity* (New York, 1931); *World Intangible* (New York, 1934); *Diversity in Holiness* (New York, 1937).

Vincent McNabb.[12] To say, as one should, that Fr. McNabb combines the qualities of Leen, Boylan and Steuart is to give a reasonably accurate notion of the man's exceptional worth.

A person who in many ways is similar to the wonderful Fr. McNabb, Cyril Martindale has apparently turned out to have been an innovator without any followers. Endowed with a marked literary flair and an uncommon narrative sense, he reintroduced a distinctive spiritual genre into the 20th century: namely, the lives of the saints as vehicles of doctrinal instruction.[13] It is a genre with its dangers, as previous centuries have given more than ample witness. But in Fr. Martindale's hands it produced nothing but good, probably because his mind was so stocked with learning and his life itself was so rich in priestly experience. Unaccountably, what he wrote in this distinctive way seems not to have enjoyed a continuing popularity. Equally deserving of a continuing popularity, and apparently not getting it, have been the collections of his doctrinal sermons[14] as well as his writings—pioneers of a sort—on the liturgy.[15] A Martindale renaissance is long overdue.

When he put his mind to it, Fr. Martindale was a literary stylist of the first order; that his style was of the 19th century rather than the 20th is, under the circumstances, irrelevant. Ronald Knox, on the other hand, could write in the style of any century, and he did. It is this phenomenal ability, loudly envied by his secular contemporaries who were themselves trying to

[12] *Oxford Conferences on Prayer* (St. Louis, 1904): revised edition, *The Science of Prayer* (London, 1936); *The Craft of Prayer* (London, 1935); *In Our Valley* (London, 1938).

[13] Among others: *In God's Army* (New York, 1914-1915); *Upon God's Holy Hills* (New York, 1920); *The Vocation of Aloysius Gonzaga* (St. Louis, 1928); *From Byeways and Hedges* (London, 1935); *What Are Saints?* (London, 1936).

[14] *The Kingdom and the World* (St. Louis, 1928); *The Wounded World* (St. Louis, 1929); *The Creative Words of Christ* (New York, 1930); *Christianity Is Christ* (New York, 1935); *Our Blessed Lady* (New York, 1939).

[15] *The Mind of the Missal* (New York, 1929); *The Words of the Missal* (New York, 1932); *The Prayers of the Missal*, 2 vols. (New York. 1936-1937); *Towards Loving the Psalms* (New York, 1940).

live by their pens, which makes it difficult to assess him as a spiritual writer. The delight one has with his way of saying something can prevent one's inquiring into what he is really saying. If one excludes what he himself considered his *magnum opus,* the historical *Enthusiasm,*[16] the only things of a spiritual nature which we have are his published sermons. In them style is paramount. Each is an essay meticulously written and re-written before being delivered. The result is twofold. First, one meets not the man but his dictionary. Secondly, what he says is what he was expected to say. Not surprisingly, then, although there was so much of it in his own life, there is no *Angst* in Knox's sermons. Yet, if one passes over his *Occasional Sermons*[17] (which have been described as "rich carpets spread for the feet of prelates and scholars"), there is an agape, even more prominently present in his life, which everywhere pervades them.[18] And who really would argue that the manner of ex-pression, although often distracting, does not almost measure up to the message?

It is really no criticism of Gerald Vann that the message so rarely measures up to the manner of its expression. Over the years he proved himself capable of taking the most worn out sort of platitude and, by cuddling it and patting it and stroking it, have it purr like an epigram. Great was the profit in having a conventional truth so unconventionally expressed, whether it be the abiding relevance of ethics in contemporary living[19] or the relevance—social, this time—of the individual Christian[20] or simply the relevance of man himself.[21] It is far less easy to

---

[16] New York, 1950.

[17] New York, 1960.

[18] *The Window in the Wall: Reflections on the Holy Eucharist* (New York, 1956); *Bridegroom and Bride* (New York, 1957); *Pastoral Sermons* (New York, 1960); *University and Anglican Sermons* (New York, 1963); *A Retreat for Lay People* (New York, 1955); *The Priestly Life: A Retreat* (New York, 1958); *A Retreat for Beginners* (New York, 1960).

[19] *Morals Maketh Man* (New York, 1938).

[20] *The Divine Pity* (New York, 1946).

[21] *The Heart of Man* (New York, 1945).

commend his later writings, so uncritically were they placed under the then pervasive shadow of Carl Jung.[22]

The temptation is great to say that Hubert Van Zeller is a Marmion redivivus—a temptation I would gladly give in to provided that I could make a qualification or two in the process. The great, Marmion-like thing that Van Zeller does is to present the Benedictine *Pax* in all its gracious amplitude,[23] but he presents it in very much his own way. His spiritual writings are as deeply meditative and theologically robust as Marmion's: moreover even in comparison, they are distinctively innocent of all frills. Perhaps the reason lies in his being a sculptor as well as a writer. His books possess the cleanness of line and the solidity and earthiness which one associates with good stone sculpture such as he is accustomed to produce when wearing his other cap.

When one turns to the consideration of writings on spirituality by American authors, a quite marked difference leaps to the eye which is largely explainable in cultural terms. Because these writings initially rose out of a sociological milieu different from that of the British Isles, the areas that are emphasized and the techniques that are utilized are different. The readers addressed in the early part of the century were relatively recent immigrants—poor, uneducated and little informed about their religion beyond what was provided in the catechism to any youngster. Accordingly, when it came to the writing of books for them, they were treated pretty much as they were accustomed to being treated on the parish level. There the priest, usually the only educated person in the group, had to fulfill many functions for them which normally they would have been expected to fulfill for themselves. They had to pray and they had to bring the truths of their faith into relation with their environment. Therefore, books came into existence which did one or

[22] A prime example is *The Paradise Tree* (New York, 1959).
[23] His books are to be counted by the dozen, but one would particularly wish to recommend *The Inner Search* (New York, 1957), *The Holy Rule* (New York, 1958), *Approach to Penance* (New York, 1958) and *Approach to Calvary* (New York, 1961).

the other, if not both, for them. Of these the most successful and influential were the multiple small volumes by Francis Le Buffe.[24] For a long time Martin Scott also provided such a substitute spirituality.[25] In both these authors, and in the multitudinous others who sought to fulfill the same functions, there is a curious common emphasis upon the individualistic in one's Christian life which seems incapable of explanation in terms of the sociological milieu. It is most clearly exemplified by one of the most successful of Fr. Scott's books, *God and Myself.*[26] It is true that there is a brief rhetorical warrant for the expression itself discoverable in the writings of St. Augustine. But to make it one's central theme, to suggest that the primal Christian relationship is a one-to-one relationship between oneself and God, is somewhat less than happy. However, despite its stress upon the individual, the spirituality itself was not unduly introspective. Nevertheless, since it was individualistic, it was also antisocial. And if one wants to know why the Catholic Church in North America responded so poorly to the social needs obvious at the time, one will find at least part of the answer in the highly individualistic substitute spirituality which was being inserted into the minds of the most generous of Catholics. The question was not of oneself and one's neighbor under God, but simply of oneself and God.

By the 4th decade of this century the changed social and intellectual condition of most Catholics made substitute spirituality of any sort—individualistic or not—generally out of place. Nevertheless it continued to exist, mainly directed at nuns. For reasons which defy analysis, nuns were thought by these eager authors to have been somehow frozen in the situation of their immigrant forebears—uneducated and little informed about their religion and needing someone to do their praying and thinking for them. The resultant large and financially profitable essay in the unreal continues with only the slightest abatement per-

---

[24] *My Changeless Friend,* 27 vols. (New York, 1915-1943).
[25] *You and Yours* (New York, 1921); *Religion and Common Sense* (New York, 1926); *Happiness* (New York, 1931).
[26] New York, 1917.

ceptible today. It would be a service to no one at all to give
bibliographical information here about such authors as these;
their hearts, at least, seem in the right place, and decent obscurity might best cloak them wholly. Articles by nuns themselves
now are, day by day, gradually bringing about that happy consummation.[27]

One large element in the social environment of the Catholic
authors of the early part of this century was a circumambient
Protestantism of which they were constantly aware. Yet, strangely
enough, it seems to have exercised no positive influence at all
upon their spirituality. That they, an introverted cultural minor-
ity, had no impact on Protestant spirituality was perhaps only
to be expected. Yet this second absence of influence is, for the
historian, much the stranger of the two, for a type of spiritual
writing came into existence among Protestants shortly after-
ward which seems little more than a logical extension of the
sort of thing that Catholics had been producing. I have in mind
that curious religious *genre littéraire* which publishers advertise
as "self-help" books. In them extreme individualism is now
coupled with extreme optimism. Norman Vincent Peale soon
became the prolific high priest of this latter-day Pelagianism
which was—and continues to be—almost as popular among
Catholic readers as among Protestants. Only Fulton Sheen, so
far as I know, has attempted a Catholic equivalent. However,
his *Peace of Soul* [28] must be classified as a temporary aberra-
tion, characteristic less of man's constant doctrine that of his
desire, equally constant, to speak to the needs of contemporary
man. This he appears to have succeeded in doing upon a phenomenal scale throughout three decades in his published radio
and television sermons.[29] It would not be inappropriate to de-

---

[27] Their appearance in the conventional spiritual periodicals such as
Review for Religious, Sponsa Regis, Spiritual Life and *Cross and Crown*
is more than compensated by their writings in the mass circulation periodicals (50,000-350,000 circulation) such as *Commonweal, America,
Jubilee, National Catholic Reporter* and *The Sign* where happily their
knowledgeable contributions are matched by those of other women.

[28] New York, 1949.

[29] *The Moral Universe* (Milwaukee, 1936); *The Cross and the Crisis*

scribe him as a somewhat more sophisticated LeBuffe or Scott, for where they sought to do the reader's thinking for him, Bishop Sheen strives to get the reader to think for himself. Moreover, with him Catholic spirituality gained a hearing among Protestants, chiefly, it would seem, because, being a philosopher, his appeal was to the basic reasonableness common to all men. But history is full of paradoxes. The Catholic author who has far surpassed even Bishop Sheen in having his spirituality accepted by Protestants is Thomas Merton, writing within the mystery of a particular contemplative vocation. In both men, of course, distinctive literary styles have contributed to their popularity: in Sheen, a Gibbon-like clarity and an epigrammatic flair; in Merton, that springtime freshness of language possible only to authentic poets. The spiritual literary event of the 1940's was the publication of Merton's autobiography,[30] and its impact has scarcely lessened since. A good case could be made for saying that he is spiritually most convincing and helpful when, whether in that work or in its sequel,[31] he is writing about himself. Yet a very high place must be reserved for his more impersonal classics, *Seeds of Contemplation*[32] and *No Man Is an Island.*[33]

It is a long distance from LeBuffe to Merton, but there is no indication that Merton is a terminal point in American spirituality. Influences, emanating in particular from the Catholic universities, are operative today, and these influences promise to provide an even more substantial spirituality for tomorrow. The number of monographs in religious psychology, pastoral sociology and biblical spirituality is constantly on the increase. Best of all, theology is beginning to make its contribution. And

---

(Milwaukee, 1938); *Whence Come Wars?* (New York, 1940); *A Declaration of Dependence* (Milwaukee, 1941); *For God and Country* (New York, 1941); *Love One Another* (New York, 1944); *Life Is Worth Living,* 5 vols. (1953-1957).

[30] *The Seven Storey Mountain* (New York, 1948); Br. ed.: *Elected Silence* (London, 1949).

[31] *The Sign of Jonas* (New York, 1953).

[32] New York, 1949.

[33] New York, 1955.

here, in the works of Robert Gleason, we have not only promise but fulfillment.[34] His is a theology of the Christian life that is distinctively North American in its pragmatism, in its coming to grips with a present culture which is beheld in an incarnational perspective; there is no divorce between the spiritual and the temporal. Hence he provides a spirituality which makes possible and meaningful the acceptance and transformation of one's ambient culture.

[34] Cf. especially *The World To Come* (New York, 1958), *Christ and the Christian* (New York, 1959), and *To Live Is Christ* (New York, 1961).

PART III
DO-C DOCUMENTATION
CONCILIUM

Office of the Executive Secretary
Nijmegen, Netherlands

Hans Waldenfels, S.J. / *Tokyo, Japan*

Japan's Spiritual Climate and Christianity

The American and European image of the Christian mission in Japan is largely the product of non-native missionaries. The opinion of Japanese Christians has only seldom come to the attention of the Western world. Facts such as these point up the special importance of the commemorative volume prepared in honor of Father H. Dumoulin, S.J., on the occasion of his 60th birthday (May 31, 1965) by twenty-five of his Catholic colleagues, friends and students. The work entitled *Japan's Spiritual Climate and Christianity*[1] reviews the development of the Japanese Church during the intervening hundred years since the discovery of the "Nagasaki Christians" on March 17, 1865. The publication also devotes its attention to Japan's contemporary situation. Twenty years have elapsed since 1945, when for the first time in the history of the country full religious freedom was established. And today there are many indications that Japan is reverting to its own native values, as witnessed particularly in certain forms of neo-nationalism.

The list of contributors includes Bishop Johannes Sh. Itô of Niigata, five secular priests and one religious priest; three of the priests teach at universities, while the remaining three are

[1] We quote the pages of the Japanese book: J. Okada/Sh. Anzai/ K. Otani/W. Takahashi/Sh. Tsunoda (ed), Nihon no Fûdo to Kirisutokyô, Tôkyô Risôsha 1965. The book has a table of contents in German.

in parish work. The other eighteen articles were written by lay people, two of them women. By profession fifteen of these authors are university professors: five teach philosophy, three history and one each teaches political science, economics, religious sociology, esthetics and German literature. The two women are also educators. Of the remaining three authors, one is a writer, three are businessmen. Their respective ages are not given, but it would appear that the forty-to-fifty age group is most strongly represented.

The work is divided into four sections: "Theology in Adaptation", "Spiritual Contacts", "Community Life" and "The Arts Here and Abroad". Following Japanese custom H. Dumoulin concludes the book with some reflections on the Japanese mission and the universality of Christianity.

In this resume I would like to show what the book has to say about Japan's present-day intellectual and spiritual situation. I feel it might well influence the development of the rest of the world. We will also explore what the book has to say on Japan's relation to Christianity, in view of learning some of the questions Japan is likely to ask. As we will observe, Japanese Christians are more inclined to question Christianity on the basis of their deep-rooted attachment to their homeland and its pre-Christian native culture rather than to question as Christians their country's values. The majority of the authors are therefore primarily concerned with examining their own Japanese situation, trying to find their bearings and to effect the transition from the past they no longer understand to a present they have not yet fully mastered mentally and spiritually. While there are few references to the Council, there is no denying that in this book Christians are entering into an astonishingly intensive dialogue with their own world.

I

JAPAN TODAY

In the "Far West"

According to M. Yanase, S.J., we are justified in calling present-day Japan the "Far West" rather than the "Far East" (137). The profound changes in Japanese life subsequent to World War II are striking. On the surface the change is characterized by rapid development toward greater automation and mechanization, and toward increased efficiency in production through the adoption of the latest innovations. High-rise buildings are being constructed in all of Japan's cities despite the threat of earthquakes; mass communications media reach into the most remote village to mold public opinion. A majority of the Japanese population is being affected by the engulfing processes of urbanization (185). And as deplorable as it might be that since the war Japan's cities are rapidly losing their local color and today are almost vying with one another to become uniform, the fact of the matter is that today human life nowhere escapes the processes of mechanization (130). Women are not only man's equal in the field of education, but in the business world as well, where they can gain economic independence through professional work of their own (242f.). Virtually no aspect of Japanese life has been left untouched by the incursions of modern civilization (294).

Similarly the traditional way of thinking that originated in Buddhism and Confucianism is for all practical purposes extinct, especially among the middle and younger age groups. With few exceptions traditional religious ideas no longer constitute the positive norm of conduct; even intellectual interest in them is rare (128). Mikumu goes even so far as to say that the preoccupation with old Japanese traditions, which is still cultivated in many places, actually makes little sense. He feels that this is only due to Western circles seeking to solve their own indigenous problems with the aid of Eastern thought (128).

If the Japanese are losing their identity it is because they have to look for an identity in things not Japanese. Japan has has to face the fact that Western-European civilization is spreading throughout the world. It cannot deny or ignore the fact that the world is on its way to becoming one great civilization with a new organic unity (130). This is bound to have grave consequences in the question of Christian accommodation. Mikumu points to two sorts of accommodation: one points backward, the other points to the future. Christianity has to be accomplished in present-day Japan, and it is a mistake to keep dreaming of a Japan that once was but which has no future (126ff.). Hence, to the degree that the individual Japanese becomes Westernized, the "Western" character of Christianity ceases to be a problem for him (152).

Yanase, who writes about the three elements which helped mold his life—Japan, Christianity and modern science—makes the point that for him Catholic religious life blended very naturally with his daily secular life. Even as a child he went to Church, and his attendance which seemed to him quite natural became a cherished habit, although he was not baptized until he suddenly fell seriously ill sometime later (134f.). Yanase found it so "natural" because he was born into the higher strata of society (his father was a personal physician of the emperor) where Western ideas and the Western way of life are no longer completely foreign (136). However, he warns his readers not to identify this relatively thin layer with the broader middle and lower classes.

The Different Point of Departure

The first impression one has of Japan can be deceiving, and we must not jump to conclusions. Y. Inoue, a secular priest who already won notoriety through his earlier article on the "Japanization of Christianity" (in *Rise*, March, 1963), rightly insists that Japan's historical development has to be analyzed objectively. It can very well be, he says, that two people or two nations encounter one another in the same particular situation, and yet the situation is different for either of them to the degree

that their backgrounds are different. After all, one cannot interpret the historical present without regard for the historical past
(24). This is another insight of great significance on the question of accommodation. A warning is sounded against rash
action in either direction. While it would be rash to neglect the
problem of inner accommodation on account of Japan's West-
ernization, it would be equally rash to take the old Japan with
its religions and traditions so seriously that one no longer sees
the difference between what is defunct and what must be preserved for the future.

The Historical Foundation

Actually a great number of articles deal with the past and
with how to cope with it. In particular there are statements concerning the influence of Buddhism in Japan, the Japanese form
of society and the Japanese character.

(a) Buddhism

It may come as a surprise to Western readers that not Shintoism, but Buddhism, is the religion given so much attention. This
is due to the fact that Shintoism, while it has nourished Japanese life for centuries as a "State religion"—we have only to
mention the Japanese's love of nature, of mountains, of flowers,
of trees, his delight in the gay side of life, such as youth, wed-
dings, the beginning of the year—is in no way comparable to the
more solid parallel phenomena of State Churches in the West.
On the whole, Buddhism had little trouble with Shintoism,
S. Tsunoda says; Shintoism was tenuous in its religious doctrine
and did not offer much resistance to Buddhism's conceptions
about man and world (64).

But why is the influence of Buddhism also on the wane? The
reason, Tsunoda maintains, is that the popular Amida Buddhism has strayed too far away from the ethics and the asceticism of traditional Buddhism (71f.). Unfortunately, he neglects
to show what part the traditional Japanese social forms had in
this transformation. In a certain sense, however, Tsunoda con-

firms the warning G. Rosenkranz made a few years ago. In the course of its history Buddhism has lost much of its effectiveness because it was less successful in making Japan Buddhist than it was in becoming Japanized itself.[2] This raises the question of how far accommodation to regional peculiarities can go before a religion runs the risk of losing its own identity.

Another article broaches the subject of language. A great number of basic human words such as suffering, sin, death, truth, knowledge, origin, relation and others take on a different meaning or at least a different shade of meaning according to their various religious origins. In a dialogue with people coming from a culture with strong Buddhist influences, one cannot take the meaning of certain terms for granted, especially not in the age of the dialogue when thorough comparative studies (of semantics) are regarded as imperative (112ff.). Unfortunately, missing from the book are analyses of the relations between Zen and Christianity or of mysticism and Christian revelation. All we learn about these subjects is by way of minor, marginal remarks.

(b) *The Japanese Form of Society*

More than in the area of religion, the Japanese tradition appears to retain its effectiveness in subliminal social attitudes —although profound changes are taking place here, too. First of all one has to distinguish the various classes of society. As everyone knows, the relatively thin layer of the upper classes has been amenable to Western thinking for almost a hundred years now, decidedly more so than are the rest of the people. But while the class differences are so radical that the upper class has long been considered untypical of the average Japan, today the masses are slowly making the adaptation.

Throughout its long history, Japanese society was essentially determined by the larger family, the "house". This family was originally rural, rigidly hierarchical in structure and self-support-

[2] See *Zeitschrift für Theologie und Kirche* 58 (1961), p. 389.

ing, i.e., exclusive. Today this type of social bond is breaking down; and the effects of the subsequent disintegration can be seen even in the villages, where a majority of the able-bodied population, men and women alike, are looking for financial betterment in the cities (193ff.). Mass media does the rest (186).

Yet remnants of the old large family social order can still be observed in industrial companies both large and small. According to J. Okada, a professor of economics, the relation between traditionalism and modern efficiency is in many cases rather unbalanced (180, also 232ff.). Behind the guise of a "humane working climate" often lies the conception of the ancient, emotionally charged, hierarchical grand-family with its father, oldest son and attendant lineage. It is striking to see to what extent the company still encroaches on the private life of its employees; it intervenes, for example, even in matters of marriage (180f.). Frequently there is a tendency to exclusiveness and to form clans or cliques. This sharply restricts the development of personal freedom and responsible independence (182f.). This has its effect on personnel policies where recruiting is concerned, and promotions are often made with no consideration of achievement or qualification. A free choice of jobs and liberty of movement are still rather limited or at least considered to be not in keeping with Japanese feeling. It will be a long time before this attitude is changed (184f.).

It goes without saying that the strong social ties that bind the Japanese to either family or—today—to his company make conversion to Catholicism very difficult, since conversion always means that an individual has to emancipate himself from these norms.

(c) *The Japanese Character*

The strongest manifestation of what still remains truly Japanese is the national character. In his article "Japan's Spiritual Climate and Christianity", Father Inoue makes a thorough study of the typical Japanese way of experiencing the reality around him. But he fails to mention to what extent traditional religious insight and experience might have some aftereffect.

There is no doubt that it is not abstract, readily communicable perception which is of primary importance to the Japanese, but rather that "perception on the basis of encounter" which resists communication through concepts (27). But to preclude any misconception we have to add immediately that this "encounter" must not necessarily be an encounter between persons. This is quite evident if we are aware of the part beauty plays in this particular mode of knowledge. Inoue asks: "Might it not be its awareness of beauty that provides the foundation for the Japanese sense of morality and value?" (30). But again, according to S. Endô the Japanese sense of beauty is not identical with that of the West. Endô makes his point: "The Japanese finds a flower that is odorless more beautiful than one with fragrance" (250).

This directs our attention to another point that several authors explain through recourse to some short poems of Bashô (1644-94), a famous poet well grounded in the world of Zen.

> See the ancient lake,
> into it plunges a frog—
> sound but of water.

The translation, even if it conforms to the Haiku meter (5-7-5 syllables), is hardly good; for it is only adequate if it conveys what the poet wants to express: not the view of a landscape, or the frog he sees or the sound he hears, but the silence he experiences when he hears the sound of the water (33).

The Japanese loves nature. But "that does not mean so much that he loves the individual things in nature; what he loves is the stream of existence which pervades and permeates things to the ground of their being, or just the beauty of the harmony which embraces all things" (32f.). The Japanese is attracted to the non-verbal and mysterious that loses its depth in the delimiting concept (251). Hence the Japanese preference for the intuitive, for the suprarational, for feeling (36ff.). The Japanese is at home in meditation, and such biblical words as "taste", "perceive", "behold", "rejoice", "know" and others are more natural to him and affect him more profoundly than they do the rationalistic Westerner. It still remains to be seen, however, whether and how scientific thinking and intuitive-meditative perception will ever form a unique synthesis (139).

II

JAPAN AND CHRISTIANITY

In the following pages we will point out some of the difficulties facing Christianity in Japan and for which Christianity is not itself responsible. Everything traditional that still has an unconscious hold on the Japanese people will—to the degree that it goes unrecognized—offer resistance to missionary work and to Christianity's dialogue with Japan.

Religious Liberty

Religious liberty is distinctly enunciated in the Meiji Constitution of 1889. But the traditional form of society which held the individual captive was detrimental to the propagation of Christianity. The intellectuals were the first to break with this tradition. This explains why Christianity enjoyed its initial success within these circles when it inaugurated its second missionizing campaign. Anyone else who became a Christian made himself a social outcast (187f.). This might also explain why Christianity did not produce any significant spiritual leaders— apart from K. Uchimura (1861-1930), whose idea of a non-denominational Christianity is still effective in Japan to this day (188). Not until the social traditions began to break down after World War II did true religious liberty become a reality, at least in the larger cities. This liberty will continue to increase as the freedom to enter new social relationships (in education, in professional life, etc.) increases. On the other hand, the Church will have to make a greater effort than it has in the past to form a genuine community life of its own in order to withdraw the individual Christians from their isolation (189).

Another question is whether the Church ought not give more freedom to that modicum of community life that already exists. A one-sided emphasis on the parish system could in the long run be extremely anachronistic, especially in Japan. It could conceivably hamper the formation of natural Christian communities on other than the parish level, for example, in the large companies (189).

Historical Objections to Christianity

Church recognition of a true pluralism, which also gives full scope to free competition in the realm of ideas, might render useless many of the old objections made against Christianity in Japan. But there are still some lingering ill effects dating back to the end of Japan's first one hundred years of Christianity. The first Christian missionaries had certainly made a good impression. They were educated, open-minded men who had received their training at the best schools in Europe (212). But when the notion gained ground that Christianity with its aspirations toward universality threatened the unity of the Japanese empire, the initial sympathy turned into distrust, fear, antipathy and eventually rejection (214).

This led to persecution and the suppression of Christianity and—what is even more consequential—to the total isolation of Japan from the rest of the world. Restricted trade was maintained only with China, Korea, the Ryûkyû Islands and with Holland (216). The foreigners, Chinese and Dutchmen, who were admitted to Japan, were given detailed instructions on where to stay in the port of Nagasaki, and all the dealings with the Ryûkyû Islands were done by Japanese citizens (216).

Quite possibly the strict observance of the old social rules dates back to the period immediately following the period of persecution; it was certainly much intensified by the controls that were rigorously carried out during that time. If one former Christian was discovered, his progeny was usually on the lists of unreliable personages for surveillance through four generations (217).

The treatment of the Dutch comprises a chapter in itself. They were ridiculed in every conceivable manner to prevent their becoming in any way attractive to the Japanese. Z. Sakuma (1811-64) coined the slogan: "Eastern customs—Western technology." The idea was to take over scientific and technological progress from the West without committing oneself to Western values and ideology (220). It was partly owing to this attitude —still very prevalent at the beginning of Japan's modern era— that the country went through a process of modernization in such a brief time, while in the same period Christianity was unable to make comparable headway among the social classes.

In this connection the article of F. Naganos on the influence of Christianity on the literature of the Meiji period should be mentioned; the author comes to the conclusion that the accusation of apostasy from Christianity which is often brought against many of the writers of that time is ultimately unfounded. In order to prove true apostasy, the author rightly observes, there first has to be true conversion; the fact that a person is baptized is not necessarily evidence of his true conversion (266). Those men, for example Tôkuku Kitamura (1868-94), Kunikida Doppô (1871-1908), Tôson Shimazaki (1872-1943), Takeo Arishima (1878-1923) and others, became acquainted with Christianity in a Western language, primarily in English, and in the form of Puritan Protestantism, and their encounter was largely emotional. They were not aware of the fact that this severe, almost anticultural and extreme (because it stressed transcendence in a one-sided manner) form of Christian monotheism was bound to lead them into trouble with their own culture and that a true conversion would first require a rational confrontation with Japanese history. It thus becomes understandable why joining and leaving Church-organized Christianity followed each other so rapidly. In most cases it did not take long for the emotional monism to assert itself again, which feels that "man and god", "one and god", "gods", "nothing and the heavens" are only different names for the same single reality (267f.).

Answers that Are Not Understood

The reference to monotheism, which makes God an object in a face-to-face encounter with man (268), leads us to those basic questions that usually fail to get sufficient attention in Christian instruction. But these are problems of such importance that their renewed rethinking is definitely called for.

Before the typically Christian elements of our message will be understood, two points will have to be clarified: the question of God and of God's relation to man and the world. This takes us into a fundamental theology especially suited to the Japanese mentality. And because it takes the listeners into consideration it is bound to be more attractive and understandable than our previous attempts.

Almost none of the catechisms presently in use in Japan try to prepare the terrain for religious insight by reflecting on the ways in which different mentalities approach the subject of God. They plunge right into proving the existence of God and clarifying his attributes, without questioning whether the student really knows what is meant by the term "God" or even whether he has any genuine interest in the question. It is taken for granted he does. Otherwise the treatise on God would not be preceded by the question: "What or who is God?" K. Kasuya is right in pointing out that man must first be convinced that the question is worth asking before he gets involved with the evidence of God's existence (17f.). Moreover the Japanese is very sensitive to the mystery and the depth behind everything. He should therefore be shown at the very outset that Christianity is "the mystery never fully expressed through the deficient medium of words" (76). The correct point of departure is first to introduce the Japanese to the mystery. Typically, even in a strictly sociological study by S. Anzai, an almost insignificant mysterious experience such as a dream about the mother of God is described as having occasioned missionary activity in the particular area being studied (199f.).

It is no coincidence that K. Otani discovers Eastern elements in the negative theology of Dionysius the Pseudo-Areopagite

(157ff.). Otani goes along with the Areopagite in preferring negative theology to a positive one, the *apophasis* to *kataphasis* (159). Otani's suggestion that there might have been direct links between the neo-Platonic forefathers of negative theology and the East merits closer investigation (162ff.). It is a fact that in Japan practically no theological attention has been given the concept of "nothingness" which is so significant in Japanese Buddhist thinking (164f.).[3] The difficulty of these problems should not deter us from studying them intensively; the problems are much more open to discussion in Japan than they appear to be in the West. Inoue, for example (and I personally agree with him on this point), speaks out against condemning the religious philosophy of the Japanese and their sense of the cosmos as pantheistic (38); but this is precisely what two other Japanese authors do in the book (122ff; 251ff.).

One of the reasons why the Christian concept of God is so widely misunderstood by non-Christians is the exaggerated emphasis we place on God's transcendence, at the expense of the divine immanence in the world (40). Partly to blame no doubt is our rationalistic presentation of the proofs of God's existence. It gives the dangerous impression that we presume to handle God as we would a thing. A number of the authors point out new ways of talking about God that would be more amenable to the Japanese intellectual character. For example, Inoue describes "perception through encounter" as being more to Japanese taste (40); Kasuya tries to elaborate an approach to God which starts with an *a priori* knowledge of man (14ff.); Sakuma, in a study on the German mystic Eckhardt, seeks to show the priority of experience and—in Scholastic terms—the "cognitio connaturalis" over reflection (78ff.). Inoue writes: "It is true what Maritain says: whoever touches being, touches God. If the experience which Bashô and others describe is an existential experience in which we encounter existence, is it unreasonable to think that what Bashô came in contact with was ultimately God himself?

[3] See H. Waldenfels, "Absolute Nothingness. Preliminary Considerations on a Central Notion in the Philosophy of K. Nishida and the Kyôto School," *Monumenta Nipponica* 3/4 (1966).

If, however, God is the personal God who revealed himself in Jesus Christ, should we not rather demonstrate God at that particular level where the existential experience of the Japanese has been surpassed? [4]

Also closely associated with the question of God is that of creation. Replying to an objection made by the famous D. T. Suzuki, M. Matsumoto, a philosopher, treats the problem of creation *ex nihilo* with a profound knowledge of Scholasticism; the problem, Matsumoto says, is seldom correctly understood, even by those who do not avoid the effort of hard thinking. However, this is not the place to elaborate on the question.

All this goes to show that there are still some very vital questions which remain either unanswered or have been answered inadequately. Here again we are concerned with the problem of theological language and different ways of thinking.

The Way of Thinking

S. Kôyoma energetically disputes the adoption of Scholastic methods. The German philosopher R. V. Koeber (1848-1923), who as the teacher of numerous Japanese philosophers strongly influenced the study of philosophy in Japan, urgently called for the study of the Greek and Latin classics, since in his opinion they were indispensable for an authentic understanding of philosophy (142). Kôyama also agrees with many Japanese scholars that it is within the framework of Western philosophy that the philosophy of Japan has found its own form. But then the question arises: How deeply has one to delve into the sources of a philosophy in order to understand it? But is not neo-Scholasticism in its historical origin a counter-movement against secularized modern thinking? Neo-Scholasticism arose in the shadow of modern ideas to obstruct modern developments. In a country like Japan which imports both Western enlightenment and neo-

[4] Here the question could be asked whether the purely objective, rational foundation of faith should not be at least supplemented by pointing up ways to a personal decision and by giving full consideration to man's directedness toward this world, and this in the training of priests as well as in catechesis.

Scholastic anti-enlightenment, the *anti*-movement is at a definite disadvantage (142f.).

Another point worth considering is this: True, Japan's openness to modern technology and material progress in the Meiji period was eventually followed by an openness to the historical and spiritual values of the West (144). But this latter development was extremely short lived. The end of World War II seems to mark the end of European centrism. What has emerged in the world since then is a tendency toward a pluralism of ideological and political leadership which replaces the monism of a European-centered history. Kôyama asks whether in view of this historical turning point Japan ought to cease surrendering to Europe because it can no longer lead to participating in the central current of world history (146). And must not neo-Scholasticism (Kôyama principally has in mind neo-Scholasticism as it appears in Japan, but includes such people as Maritain in his denunciation) be charged with unhistorical thinking in this regard (147)?

The author's arguments lack conviction insofar as he is not aware of the historical implications of the incarnation of Christ and so fails to see the permanent role which the Occident has in passing on the Christian message and the reality it implies.[5]

The article by K. Kasuya on the encounter of East and West in theology and philosophy shows the other side of the coin. While Kôyama is mainly impressed with the pluralism of the modern world, Kasuya sees, from a theological-christological as well as a philosophical-historical perspective, the ultimate unity of the world and of mankind. He is aware of the necessity of using an initially anthropological approach (16f.); he is aware of every man's longing for God (17f.) and he knows of the breakthrough of Christ's subjective action into the objective world that was achieved in the paschal mystery of the Lord (19) and of the possibility of man's implicitly apprehending and affirming that divine economy in which he has been implicated

---

[5] See K. Rahner, "Abendland, II. Zur Theologie des Abendlandes," in *Lexikon für Theologie und Kirche* I, 18-21.

from the first moment of his creation (20). A Zen master was once asked how one could retrieve a lost experience. The master answered: "Your question is like the question of the man who sits on the back of the ox and asks: 'Where is the ox?'" (20). This is true of our concrete life. Whoever understands this ultimate unity of mankind in Christ also respects the necessity and the positive nature of multiplicity. He will rediscover it in Christ in an ever new and creative way, and he will tell of it, since the multiplicity of the world is part of the rich fullness of Christ. Only when viewed from this perspective would a criticism of neo-Scholasticism become justified.

This is the place to point out the ambiguity involved when different authors speak of a "Japanization" of Christianity. The term certainly has a correct sense. Tsunoda, for example, says: "It means nothing but the Christianization of Japanese culture." (63) But in historical perspective we ought not forget that the "Japanization of Buddhism" meant something more, namely, a removal of essential doctrinal content if it should happen not to be to the liking of the Japanese mentality. A "Japanization of Christianity" must not lead to a similar surrender of Christianity. In this event Christianity would cease to be the "salt of the earth" for Japan; neither could it demand that metanoia of the heart which is required of every man. This constitutes one of the limits for any "de-Westernization" of Christianity.

Call for a Dialogue with the World

The contemporary Japanese attitude—in spite of many prejudices which either persist or which have been newly imported from the West—is not really hostile toward Christianity. What makes the access to Christianity so difficult for the Japanese is the fact that Christianity seems to have so little to do with everyday, secular life (132). Due to its emphasis on inner values, the other world and a renunciation of worldly things, Christianity appears rather close to the other, traditional religions which are currently without significant influence. "Modern man—and the Japanese are no exception—is without doubt more interested in social problems and tasks than in the inner piety of the individual, more in shaping this world than in the attainment of happiness in the next. Man is searching for principles to build up society rather than for an individual morality, more for peace on earth than for salvation in heaven. If Christianity is nothing but a code of private morals and a religion of the hereafter, its future appears dark—and not only in Japan" (132).

Christianity will therefore have to emphasize, more than it did heretofore, what distinguishes it from other religions (133). It will have to focus on the historical event of the incarnation of Christ, and it will have to avoid the impression that it is only a theory about God and creation. It will have to give the Japanese people its interpretation of life in this world. As Professor Y. Kobayashi correctly observes, present-day man wants to understand more about himself than ever before, more about his age and the country in which he lives. Man today only too acutely experiences human greatness and human jeopardy (170). He lives for his work and for his pleasure, yet he wonders what the basic meaning and the mission of his life might be (171). It must not come to the point where religion only calls man out of his world to take him to church, to divine service, to stillness, from the profane to the holy, isolating him more and more from his world (171). Religion must dedicate itself consciously to its tasks pertaining to human society. To accomplish this, religion will have to become aware of its own social character (Catholicism of its own ecclesiological character) (173, also 188-90). Kobayashi sees the greatest danger in an individualism of personal salvation, because this makes religion neglect its societal mission and appreciably weakens the desire to influence modern society (173). And this would mean leaving the wide area of social formation to the anti-religious or a-religious, to "isms" and ideologies (172f.).

This is true for Japan's politics, especially where it concerns economic policy and the method of handling social problems. A direct Catholic apostolate is certainly important in Japan: liturgical reform, deliberations about more adaptation to Japanese habits and customs are necessary (227). But even more important is that the Church make its contribution so that contemporary Japan might one day find the right attitude toward such problems as development and underdevelopment, capitalism and socialism, industrialization, the relation of tradition to modernity (222f.). The Church should train leaders for the workers' movement, take a position in favor of just remuneration, speak out on population and family planning (229).

All these requests are in line with the flood of worldwide inquiries directed to Vatican Council II, leading to what was at first called Schema XIII. Japan deliberately joins the chorus of nations. It can no longer live in insular isolation; Japan must feel that it is a part of the world as a whole (229). That is why the catholicity of the Church must be especially emphasized in Japan today; this alone will make the Church radiant and attractive.

In his conclusion H. Dumoulin points in this same direction. The book was dedicated to him, and it was he who through his practical work as well as his personal attitude inspired many of the ideas the book contains. Dumoulin makes the nexus to Vatican II. He knows from his own conversations that Pope John XXIII's personality made a very deep impression on a group of leading Japanese Buddhists on November 18, 1962. He is sure that an open-door theology, which gratefully affirms the latitude of the divine plan of salvation and includes all men of goodwill in the scope of divine grace, will eventually win the day for Japan (293ff.). As Christianity faces the present and opens itself to the future, as it builds bridges over the gaps of hopelessness through faith in the Lord, it will also win influence in a country like Japan. It is not theoretical doctrine that will lead the way into the future, but a brotherly participation in the daily experience and the cares of life. That is where the incarnation of Christ is happening today. It opens an avenue to knowledge of Christ, not in conceptual indoctrination, but in the encounter of Christian love.

Roger Aubert / *Louvain, Belgium*

Renewal of Monastic Life: The Brothers of the Virgin of the Poor

The modern world is often disconcerted by the monastic life and questions the meaning of the existence of monks who voluntarily isolate themselves from the world and do not share the creative activity of mankind in its quest for progress. However, though it is entirely normal for this type of vocation to pose a problem for the active—and, all too often, driven—man of the 20th century, there is something disquieting about the kind of reaction it often provokes. In his preface to the work which has occasioned this short article, Father Six frankly emphasizes this point:

> Let monks—my brothers—realize that this questioning is not always something positive like a shock that awakens us to a better understanding of realities; it is often simply indifference and an easy way of rejecting some aberrant existence. And there is no doubt that you must question yourselves here and now, asking whether your existence, such as it is, in this monastery, in this priory, in this hermitage, gives scandal in the vigorous and truthful manner of the cross of Christ—thus causing shock and clearing a path—or whether it provokes irritation in the manner of a dried-up fruit without sap like the sterile fig tree of the Gospel. Do you experience the *only God* in your life with

such an intense faith that you become a light on a mountain for the world? Or is he simply a hidden refuge in the mountain—a refuge that you monopolize for yourselves alone and from which you exclude all others?

As a matter of fact, many monks have already asked themselves this question over a long period of time—a question which basically entails discussing the entire state of monasticism today. It is no longer a secret that there exists a real crisis for monasticism, a crisis that takes on diverse forms in different countries but in the main comes down to the same key question: Are not today's monasteries excessively stamped with the medieval tradition they have inherited? Does not the burden of this tradition, which was formulated during the age of feudalism in an agricultural economy, prevent classical monasticism from continuing to fulfill the spiritual aspirations of the men of our day? These include not only those who feel called to lead a life in conformity with the original monastic ideal, but also those who, without experiencing such a vocation, still feel the need—when confronted with the life of monks—at least to hear "the call of the hero" of which Bergson spoke, and they declare themselves defrauded.

Attempts have been made on various sides to overcome this crisis and to combine the feudal Middle Ages and the old regime on one side with the evangelical aspirations of the Egyptian monks of the time of St. Antony and Pachomius or the first disciples of St. Benedict and St. Columban on the other. It is one such attempt among others which, after the experience of some ten years, is brought to the attention of the public at large through the pages of a slender volume that deserves our attention for its spiritual content, no matter what future may be in store for the concrete experiment whose charter it wishes to represent.[1]

On January 21, 1956, three monks who had come from

[1] *Au coeur même de l'Eglise. Une recherche monastique: les Frères de la Vierge des Pauvres*, with a preface by Jean-François Six (Paris-Brussels, 1966).

Belgium, under the guidance of a Benedictine of Mont-César (Louvain), settled in a glade of the Landais forest to the south of Bordeaux, about three miles from the village of Pontenx-les-Forges. In that area, next to a chapel dedicated to St. John the Baptist, there were some old abandoned farmhouses which the three "brothers" rented. "They found them almost bare. The neighbors had provided some strictly necessary furniture: a few chairs, a table, a closet; a vacation colony had loaned them beds. For installation material, the three brothers had only the contents of their valises" (p. 195). The "Brotherhood of the Virgin of the Poor" had been born.[2]

The brotherhood responded to the desire of its founders to lead a monastic life which would be closer to the ideal of the Fathers of the Desert than that of the classical monasteries—at the same time adapting this ideal to the material conditions and spiritual needs of our time. Struck by the paradoxical fact that, although the signs of a monastic renewal have been multiplying for a century, the present world is more and more disconcerted by this type of religious life, they intend to live this ideal no longer in an ivory tower but inserted in the daily life of their

[2] *Brotherhood:* to emphasize—in better fashion than the complex hierarchical organizations of the large orders—the "brotherly love" to which is dedicated a long chapter of the rule that begins with the words: "Every brotherhood is organized in such a manner that community life really takes on a brotherly character; the small number of brothers, the spiritual paternity of the father—all contribute to this" (p. 153). Brotherhood of the *Virgin of the Poor:* in order to place the new foundation under the patronage of the Virgin "who brings us Jesus and teaches us to bring him to others, like herself, in the joy of the Holy Spirit, without words, by our presence which is silent and impregnated with him" (p. 19; the patron feast of the brotherhood is celebrated on July 2, the day of the Visitation), so as also in this way to underline the importance attached to a life of real poverty. The name is inspired by that of Notre-Dame de Banneux in the diocese of Liège, though far transcending it, as explained by a note in the rule: "It is the name that [the Virgin] was pleased to give herself when she appeared in 1933 to a poor uncultured child on the high plateau of Banneux-Notre-Dame. Although her message, which is reducible to very few words, happily corresponds with the ideal of the brotherhood, it is above all because of our desire for a life of real poverty that we have chosen Mary as our mother under this title" (pp. 19-20, footnote 2).

contemporaries. They wish to be poor—not merely canonically but in reality—in the midst of the poorest of all, with no distinguishing feature from their neighbors—whether clothing, ceremonial or habit—which does not truly respond to the exigencies of their vocation as monks.

In the search for this adaptation of the monastic ideal for all times to the conditions of modern life, they were particularly inspired by that Trappist of old who would be ill at ease among the Trappists of our day, Charles de Foucauld, as well as by the spiritual and missionary current which has developed in his wake for half a century and is associated primarily—though not exclusively—with the name of Father Voillaume. It is easily understandable then that Father Jean-François Six, professor at the Seminary of the Mission of France and author of one of the better lives of Charles de Foucauld, should be the person to introduce their rule. In a few lucid words he explains how the Brothers of the Virgin of the Poor desire to be at the same time children of the monks of the East and disciples of the message of the hermit of Tamanrasset:

If we consider Charles de Foucauld, we see that he did not really grasp the Trappist life, nor did he succeed in becoming part of it; on the other hand, neither was he a missionary working with others—both priests and laymen—for evangelization. A solitary figure who never had companions, he founded neither monastic community nor missionary society. As prophet and precursor, he falls somewhere between the two and forces monks and missionaries to rediscover their own vocation in its profundity and to live in ecclesial unity. Such—it seems to me—is his place.

In like manner do the *Little Brothers* [of Father Voillaume] by their poverty and presence in the world force those of us who are missionaries to work more in the world wherein lies our task for the Church. By their life have they not invited a number of diocesan priests engaged in missionary work as well as priests of the *Mission of France* to

perform in better fashion the work entrusted to them by
the Church? Similarly, there exist Trappists and Benedic-
tines for whom Charles de Foucauld and the *Little Brothers*
have been a demanding sign: a sign that has not allowed
them to quit their monastery but has inserted them even
more in their monastic vocation and invited them to renew
it from within. For such is our condition: we must constantly be born again of the Spirit both in our lives and in
our modes of living, and we are forever in need of the Spirit
and our brothers in order to achieve this.

It is in this framework that I believe the *Brothers of the
Virgin of the Poor* can be situated. Charles de Foucauld
and his *Little Brothers* have forced them to exist as monks
in the most profound way possible. They are children of
the monks of the Desert and closely related to the monks
of the East. They desire, as one of them stated in simple
fashion, "to live what the missionaries proclaim"; they thus
remind those of us who are missionaries that our temptation
lies in forgetting to live what we proclaim or, graver still,
in forgetting what we must proclaim and reducing the missionary realization to the flesh-and-blood construction of
the human world, thus trampling upon the total destiny of
mankind. They desire to exercise the role of ambassadors
of the Christ of the last day within the Church of today and
its missionary project, and they especially wish to remind
themselves and others without ceasing that the catholicity of
the Church demands of each individual, and above all of
the monk, that he lead an open and all-embracing existence
and not a life which is petty and niggardly, withdrawn into
oneself, closed and banal (pp. 10-11).

Beginning with three members ten years ago, the Brothers
of the Virgin of the Poor now number thirty-five, belonging to
ten different nationalities and divided into five brotherhoods.
Two are found in France. The first is the Novitiate-Brotherhood
at the birthplace of the movement, Pontenx, where the brothers

live like the lowest of their Landais neighbors, cultivating their kitchen-gardens or working as salaried farmers during the hours not taken up with the divine office and their religious formation. The other is the Brotherhood of Studies established at Pontigny next to the Seminary of the Mission of France, where the brothers take courses in accord with a program adapted to the needs and capabilities of each, whether or not they are called to the priesthood.

Since 1958, a brotherhood which today comprises eight Africans among some ten brothers has been open at Rwanda; here, also, an original effort of Africanization has been pursued for the last six years: the office is not merely chanted in the language of the region to melodies of the country; it is accompanied by a great deal of bodily participation in the attitudes of the soul, to the rhythm of tambourines and the beat of handclapping. Similarly, to fill the Bantu need to crystallize thoughts into words, the brothers have the opportunity of expressing their thoughts and disclosing themselves in the "councils" wherein each can "speak his heart" spontaneously.[3]

The brothers at Rwanda live in little huts made out of straw and clay like the other huts of the country. Likewise, the Chilean brotherhood, founded in April, 1960, in the diocese of Valdivia, and the German brotherhood, established in the diocese of Hildesheim, in a region with a Protestant majority and among refugees chased from the Eastern frontiers, are established in a little rented house which is in no way distinguished from the most modest of the surrounding homes. Here the brothers, living from the fruit of their toil, lead a laborious and hidden life in imitation of Jesus of Nazareth. They exercise no direct apostolate among the populace, despite the scarcity of priests, in simple witness to the Gospel and in solidarity with the crude and diffi-

[3] For other analogous attempts at adapting the monastic life to the specific traits of the African psychology, see the report of Dom Jean Leclercq, "Le monachisme africain et le monachisme antique," in *Irénikon* 38 (1965), pp. 33-56. As the title suggests, the author stresses the numerous similarities between the Bantu aspirations and the kind of life—of prayer and spirituality—of the monks of the early Christian centuries.

cult life led by their neighbors, habitually maintaining silence and reciting the office each day.

We might also add that in the vicinity of the brotherhoods have been erected hermitages where the brothers go in turn to make their monthly recollection and their annual retreat; finally, a sisterhood of *Little Sisters* was established in January, 1960, near Pontenx by the Bishop of Dax.

The ideal that was more or less glimpsed at the beginning has gradually been rendered more precise through experience, and a first draft of the rule has been drawn up. It is still a long way from being perfectly in focus—in form or even content. Certain passages seem rather banal—although in this sphere as in others the banalities involved are not considered bad to repeat. In any case, the brothers have let themselves be persuaded that this text which attempts to express their aspirations and first realizations might be useful—just as it stands—to others engaged in an analogous quest, and after a good many hesitations they have authorized its publication.

The rule is divided into two main sections: reflections on the three vows of religion—preceded by a few pages on "solitude in the desert" and "redemptive penance"—and a draft on the concrete manner in which the brothers conceive the organization—most flexible throughout—of the life of prayer and charity.

An interesting document that should be placed in the dossier on the contemporary monastic renewal, this volume constitutes at the same time stimulating reading for every Christian—religious, priest and especially layman—who desires to live more authentically as a Christian. For, to cite another sentence from the writer of the preface, this rule "suggests and does not impose itself; it points to the Gospel rather than to remedies; it is a humble interrogation rather than a sum of principles" (p. 11). It is precisely because of this fact that it deserves to receive attention, even apart from the monastic milieux properly so called.

Even apart from the monastic milieux? Indeed, yes; first of all, because a sincere meditation on the evangelical exigencies is always justified, even for those who believe their vocation is to work in the world rather than to retreat into the desert; secondly, because the reading of this little volume will help to pose anew the very vast problem of the meaning of monasticism in the Church—in more exact terms and apart from superficial difficulties.

For many lay Christians who are enthusiastically engaged in their lay and apostolic vocation, all retreat from the world appears to be an egoistical flight in the face of the real responsibilities of today's Christian. Do they have reason to believe that every other form of vocation—except their own—lacks authenticity? Here is not the place to discuss the question as to whether it is not more true in our day that, while the People of God wages its difficult battle on the plain, it is useful for Moses to continue to pray on the mountain.

We will limit ourselves to the statement that this new rule aids in the better understanding of why certain men remain convinced that there is still a place in the Church today for a type of Christian life which is inspired by—and at the same time renews—the primitive monastic ideal. We can see therein a mid-20th-century version of the monastic life that is not merely detached from a certain number of anachronistic forms inherited from the old regime. What is more important, we can see therein a monastic life that is desirous of avoiding to the utmost degree all artificiality in certain types of religious "poverty" and all atrophy in certain ways of withdrawal from the world. These ultimately cause the monastic to know almost nothing concretely of what are the real problems and dramas of the world for which he prays and does penance.

BIOGRAPHICAL NOTES

MICHEL DE CERTEAU, S.J.: Born in 1925 in Chambery, France, he became a Jesuit and was ordained in 1956. He studied at Grenoble, Lyons, at the Sorbonne in Paris and at the Ecole des Hautes Etudes where he earned degrees in theology and philosophy. He earned his doctorate in the science of religion at the Sorbonne in 1960. At present he is associate director of the review *Christus,* assistant director of *Recherches de Science Religieuse* and director of the seminary at the Faculty of Theology in Paris. His published works in French include books on spirituality.

BERNARD COOKE, S.J.: Born in 1922 in Michigan, he became a Jesuit and was ordained in 1952. He pursued his studies at the Graduate School and the School of Divinity at the University of St. Louis, and the Catholic Institute and Catechetical Institute in Paris. He earned his doctorate in theology in Paris in 1956. He is professor of theology at Marquette University in Wisconsin. Among his writings are "The Body of Christ, Catholic Theological View," in *The Church as the Body of Christ* (1963), and "Synoptic Presentation of the Eucharist as Covenant Sacrifice," in *Theological Studies* 21 (1960). He is a regular contributor to *Theological Studies* and to other reviews such as *Worship* and *The Journal of Ecumenical Studies.*

ROBERT BULTOT: Born in 1929 at Charleroi, Belgium, he studied at the University of Louvain and at the Ecole des Hautes Etudes in Paris, earning doctorates in philosophy and in letters in 1960. He is engaged in research at the National Belgian Foundation for Scientific Research. He has contributed to many reviews and theological journals on the subject of spirituality, particularly on contempt for the world as shown in various persons and philosophies through the centuries.

JOSÉ-MARÍA GONZÁLEZ-RUIZ: Born May 5, 1916, he was ordained in 1939 for the diocese of Málaga, Spain. He studied at the Gregorian University and the Institut Biblique, both in Rome, earning his doctorate in theology in 1940 and a degree in sacred scripture in 1953. He taught Greek at the seminary in Seville, was stationed in a suburban Seville parish, and was professor of the New Testament at the seminary in Málaga as well as at the University of Salamanca. His published works include a number of books on St. Paul and numerous articles for biblical encyclopedias and journals.

PIERRE REGINALD CREN, O.P.: Born in 1932 in Lamballe, France, he became a Dominican and was ordained in 1958. He studied at the Dominican Faculty at Saulchoir, at the Sorbonne and at the Collège de France in Paris. He is now completing his dissertation for a doctorate in theology. He is presently a professor at the Dominican House of Studies at Arbresle and a member of the editorial board of *Lumière et Vie*. He is particularly interested in ecumenical dialogue, and he shares the activities of the St. Irénée ecumenical center in Lyons.

CHRISTIAN DUQUOC, O.P.: *See* front flap of book jacket.

ERNEST LARKIN, O.CARM.: Born in 1922 in Chicago, he became a Carmelite and was ordained in 1946. He studied at the Catholic University of America in Washington and at the Angelicum in Rome, earning his doctorate in 1954. He has taught theology at Catholic University since 1960. Among his writings is "The Role of Creatures in the Spiritual Life," in *Proceedings of the Catholic Theological Society of America* (1962).

CLAUDE J. GEFFRÉ, O.P.: Born in 1926 in Niort, France, he became a Dominican. After studying at the Angelicum in Rome and at Le Saulchoir in France, he was ordained in 1953 and earned his doctorate in theology in 1956. At present he is professor of dogmatic theology and rector of the Dominican Faculty at Saulchoir. He is a regular contributor to numerous reviews, including *Revue des Sciences philosophiques et théologiques, La Vie Spirituelle, Parole et Mission* and *Lumière et Vie*.

BALDOMERO JIMÉNEZ-DUQUE: Born in 1911 in Avila, Spain, he was ordained in 1936 for the diocese of Avila. He studied at Gregorian University in Rome, earning a doctorate in philosophy and degrees in theology and canon law. He is presently the rector of the diocesan seminary. His published works in Spanish include books on spirituality, the priesthood, St. John of the Cross and St. Teresa. He is also a frequent contributor to Spanish language reviews.

ELMER O'BRIEN, S.J.: Born in 1911 in Everett, Massachusetts, he became a Jesuit and was ordained in 1946. He studied at Harvard University, at Gregorian University in Rome and at Louvain, earning his doctorate in theology in 1950. At present he is teaching at Loyola College in Montreal. Among his published works are *The Essential Plotinus* (1964), *Varieties of Mystic Experience* (1964) and *Theology in Transition* (1965). He contributes regularly to *Theological Studies, Thought* and *Sciences Ecclésiastiques*.

HANS WALDENFELS, S.J.: Born in 1931 in Essen, Germany, he became a Jesuit and was ordained in 1963 in Tokyo. He pursued his studies at Pullach, in Tokyo and Kyoto, and in Rome where he specialized in fundamental theology and the philosophy of religion. He is presently studying in Europe and he contributes articles to Japanese reviews such as *Katorikku Shingaku* and *Monumenta Nipponica*, as well as to *Katholische Missionen, Geist und Leben* and *Stimmen der Zeit*.

ROGER AUBERT: Born January 16, 1914, in Ixelles-Bruxelles, Belgium. After ordination, he earned his doctorate in philosophy in 1933 and his doctorate in theology in 1942. He was professor in the major seminary at Malines from 1944 to 1952 when he was appointed to the University of Louvain as professor of church history. He is director of the *Revue d'Histoire Eccl.* and of the French Dictionary of Church History and Geography, vice-president of the Belgian Commission on Church History, co-director of the new *Histoire d'Eglise,* and member of many international historical societies. His numerous published works take up the subjects of Christian unity, 20th-century theology, Vatican Council II and Church history. He contributes to numerous reviews.

International Publishers of CONCILIUM

ENGLISH EDITION
Paulist Press
Glen Rock, N. J., U.S.A.

Burns & Oates Ltd.
25 Ashley Place
London, S.W.1

DUTCH EDITION
Uitgeverij Paul Brand, N. V.
Hilversum, Netherlands

FRENCH EDITION
Maison Mame
Tours/Paris, France

GERMAN EDITION
Verlagsanstalt Benziger & Co., A.G.
Einsiedeln, Switzerland

Matthias Grunewald-Verlag
Mainz, W. Germany

SPANISH EDITION
Ediciones Guadarrama
Madrid, Spain

PORTUGUESE EDITION
Livraria Morais Editora, Ltda.
Lisbon, Portugal

ITALIAN EDITION
Editrice Queriniana
Brescia, Italy